Talk Show and Entertainment Program Processes and Procedures

Multiple Camera Video Series
By Robert J. Schihl

Television Commercial Processes and Procedures

Talk Show and Entertainment Program Processes and Procedures

Studio Drama Processes and Procedures

TV Newscast Processes and Procedures

Talk Show and Entertainment Program Processes and Procedures

Robert J. Schihl, Ph.D.

Focal Press

Boston London

Library of Congress Cataloging-in-Publication Data

Schihl, Robert J.
    Talk show and entertainment program processes and
procedures / Robert J. Schihl.
        p.   cm.—(Multiple camera video series)
    Includes bibliographical references (p.   ) and index.
    ISBN 0-240-80092-3 (pbk.)
    1. Talk shows.   2. Television—Production and direction.
I. Title.   II. Series: Schihl, Robert J. Multiple camera video
series.
PN1992.8.T3S3   1991
791.45′3—dc20
                                            91-16863
                                                CIP

British Library Cataloguing in Publication Data

Schihl, Robert J.
    Talk show and entertainment program processes and
procedures.—(Multiple camera video series)
    I. Title   II. Series
    791.45

    ISBN 0-240-80092-3

Butterworth–Heinemann
80 Montvale Avenue
Stoneham, MA 02180

10   9   8   7   6   5   4   3   2   1

Printed in the United States of America

Contents

Preface

Multiple camera video production refers to those varying video projects that create the products of the multiple camera video technology. It is usually the video production associated with a studio setting. Some of the most common multiple camera studio production today includes the talk show and entertainment program production, newscast production, television commercial production, and television studio drama production (mainly soap operas and sit-coms). Of these, only the daily newscast and occasional television commercial are still being produced at local television production studios. Occasionally, local broadcasting and cablecasting facilities produce public service talk shows. Public access channels on cable systems thrive on the locally produced talk show genre.

In network television studio production, besides the daily newscasts, the continuing daily soap opera production and talk show/entertainment programs still occupy some of the busiest and most productive of the studio projects.

While the basic skills necessary for studio production remain the same across studio production genres, preproduction tasks and production roles vary immensely from one genre to another. The beginning television producer, director, and production crews need to be aware of those studio production elements that are similar across genres as well as those that differ. It is not uncommon to find well meaning beginners performing poorly in their roles across genres when principles and criteria for one genre were erroneously applied to another. Professionally, even apparently similar studio production roles across television program genres require a different mind set and, consequently, different skills application. Hence, at beginning and intermediate television production levels, awareness of the various genres and their differences encourages varying skill development and consequent employment marketability.

Academic goals for beginning television production skills are usually oriented to some form of studio operation. Therein students have the opportunity to learn all aspects of video production from the technology of the medium to the aesthetics of the final product. In some academic programs, knowledge of these concepts and skills is required before advancing to the single camera video experience. The television studio experience encompasses all phases of video *producing skills* from those of the producer to those of the director, and all phases of video *production technology* from that of the camera operator (videographer camera skills) to that of the technical director (video editing skills). Given success in the learning stages of video production, skills still need expression. The most common expression of video production skills is to engage in some form of television studio production. The talk show and entertainment program genre is a very popular beginning studio production project. Beyond a basic television studio production handbook, there is not an adequate text available to design and organize differing studio production genres. This book concentrates on producing and the production of the television studio talk show and entertainment program.

The growth of both broadcast and cable television in the United States and abroad in the 1990s shows ever increasing development and expansion. The areas of low power television (LPTV) production, the continuing increase in cable origination programming, and the introduction of high definition television (HDTV) attest to that development and expansion. The rapid fragmentation of cable and satellite television in general is spurring the proliferation of independent television production facilities and the multiplication of television studio program genres. Producers for these independently produced and syndicated programs seek from media conventions the guidelines for producing and the production of the various genres. Publishers of books on the subject of television are seeing a growing need in these areas and are responding with an increasing number of publications. These publications assist the entrepreneur in the development of video production houses and in the training of producers. What is needed by both the broadcast educator as well as the video production entrepreneur is guidance for producing and production procedures, information on video production organizational flow, and the definition of video producing and production roles.

Following the publication of my earlier book *Single Camera Video: From Concept to Edited Master* (Focal Press, 1989), I found that educators, beginning professionals, and industry reviewers alike applauded the format in which I presented the procedural, organizational, and role definition stages of the single camera video technology. I was asked why such a format was not available for multiple camera video production. Having spent more years both in broadcast education and professional production with multiple camera video production than with single camera video production, I asked myself the same question. I hope this text is the desired response.

Talk Show and Entertainment Program Processes and Procedures is intended to meet the needs of those individuals from intermediate television education to the beginning television production facility entrepreneur who needs a clear and comprehensive road map to organizing a television studio talk show/entertainment program production. This book presents the conceptual preproduction stages of program production (e.g., writing a proposal, constructing a budget, designing a studio set, and creating lighting and audio design) as well as all levels of production skill definition and organization through the director's call for a wrap to the studio production. This road map includes the thoroughness of flowcharts for all preproduction, production, and postproduction personnel roles and the specific detail of preproduction and production organizing forms that facilitate and expedite most roles throughout the process of the studio production of the television talk show/entertainment program.

In *Single Camera Video: From Concept to Edited Master* I referred to the approach I took as "a cookbook recipe approach." I have not only not regretted the comparison but have grown confirmed in the analogy. Similar to single camera video production, multiple camera video production is a process needing the guidance of a good kitchen recipe—an ordered, procedural, and detailed set of guidelines. As with a good recipe, after initial success, a good cook adjusts ingredients, eliminates some, adds others, and makes substitutions according to taste and experience with the recipe. So, too, is it with the approach taken in this text. The production organizing details covered in this text are such that after initial introduction, depending often on available personnel, studio equipment, or production time frame, preproduction and production task roles can be multiplied, combined, or eliminated—just like the ingredients in a favorite recipe.

Specifically, the approach that this text takes to multiple camera video production is one of organization. The most frequent and vociferous compliment to *Single Camera Video* is that it organizes the whole gamut of the preproduction, production, and postproduction of single camera video production. In the same way, this text is designed to organize the multiple camera video production of the television talk show/entertainment program. Books on the other television studio genres (the newscast, the television studio drama production, and the television commercial production) are also available from Focal Press in a worktext similar to this.

The process of the television talk show and entertainment program production is presented in Chapter 1 in flowchart checklist form for preproduction, production, and postproduction stages of production. For each of the three stages, producing and production personnel roles are presented, with responsibilities and obligations listed in their order of accomplishment. In Chapter 2, the processes of preproduction, production, and postproduction are presented in chronological order of production role performance. In Chapter 3, production organization forms are provided for various preproduction and production tasks. These forms are designed to facilitate the goal or producing/production requirements at certain stages of the process of producing and production. A description and glossary for each form are presented in Chapter 4 to facilitate use of the forms.

In determining the method of presenting the television talk show/entertainment program production genre in this text some choices had to be made. Production procedures had to be adapted to a learning process. The first choice was to decide the number of producing personnel and studio production crew size. The number of producing roles and studio production crew members usually is determined by the production budget and the number of available personnel (i.e., students) in an academic environment. The choice was made to create above-the-line and below-the-line staff and crew for an average size production with a minimum number of personnel. As in the analogy of a good recipe, combine, subtract, or multiply staff and crew members according to costs and availability. The industry does that too.

Another choice was to determine the level of studio hardware and technology sophistication to assume in talk show/entertainment program production. No two television studio facilities are alike, especially in academic environments. The criterion for level of hardware and technology sophistication assumed was to be aware that no matter how much or how little a studio facility has in terms of hardware and technology, the students leaving their training time in any type of production facility still have to know some point of minimal reference to the "real world" of studio talk show and entertainment program production and employment skill expectation standards. A teacher of broadcasting can easily structure this text and its approach to an individual facility. Without an ideal point of reference, it would be very difficult to structure up to a level that was not covered in this text. Students must be made aware of what to expect in a "normal" or "ideal" studio production facility and from a studio production crew. This is what I have tried to convey. I have taught studio talk show/entertainment program production from a minimal facility to a full blown state-of-the-art facility. This text is adaptable to either.

I repeat what I wrote in *Single Camera Video*. The video production industry or television studio talk show/entertainment program production is not standardized in the procedural manner in which its video products are created. This text, although it can appear to recommend standardized approaches to achieving video products, is not intended to imply that the industry or studio talk show/entertainment program production is standardized nor is it an attempt to standardize the industry or studio talk show/entertainment program production. The presentation of ordered production steps is merely academic; it is a way of teaching and learning required stages in video production. The video product is the result of a creative process and should remain that way. This text provides order and organization to television studio production for beginning producers and directors and for intermediate television teachers and students of video production. Once someone becomes familiar with the process of any talk show/entertainment production, that person is encouraged to use what works and facilitates a task and to drop or rethink those elements that do not work or no longer facilitate the task.

I am currently a full professor—both a charter and senior television faculty member—at Regent University on the grounds of the Christian Broadcasting Network, home of the Family Channel. I teach in both their School of Radio, Television, and Film, and the School of Journalism.

ACKNOWLEDGMENTS

I am indebted to many people over many years who have contributed unknowingly to this book:

To Joanne, Joel, and Jonathan for putting up with the interminable clacking of computer keys and the whine of a printer;

To my parents, Harold and Lucille, who unwittingly turned me on to television production in 1950 by purchasing our first television set;

To Dr. Marilyn Stahlka Watt, Chair, Department of Communication, Canisius College, Buffalo, New York, for introducing me to television broadcasting and making me a television producer;

To Edward Herbert and Kurt Eichsteadt, Taft Broadcasting, for giving me the chance to have my own live, local prime-time television program;

To Marion P. Robertson, Chief Executive Officer, the Family Channel, Virginia Beach, Virginia, for giving me the opportunity to work and teach in a state-of-the-art national network television facility;

To Dean David Clark, Provost George Selig, and President Bob Slosser, Regent University, Virginia Beach, Virginia, for granting me the sabbatical to write this book;

To Karen Speerstra, Senior Editor, and Philip Sutherland, Acquisitions Editor, Focal Press, Stoneham, Massachusetts, for being the most encouraging editors and friends an author could have;

To Rob Cody, Project Manager; Julie Blim, "700 Club" Producer; and John Loiseides, Photographer, Christian Broadcasting Network, Virginia Beach, Virginia, for their research assistance;

To my thousands of television students from the State University of New York at Buffalo, the State University of New York College at Buffalo, Hampton University, and Regent University, and especially to those among them whose names I see regularly on the closing credits of network and affiliate television programs—for the thrill of seeing their names.

A.M.D.G.
Robert J. Schihl, Ph.D.
Virginia Beach, Virginia
1991

Key to the Book

Creating a successful television studio production requires that many tasks at varying stages of production be performed in sequential order. Most tasks build upon one another and are interrelated with the tasks of other production personnel. The television industry has clearly defined roles for each production personnel member. This book provides a blueprint of the duties assigned to each production role. The duties of each role—producer, director, camera operator, etc.—are first presented in a checklist flowchart. Role duties are then cross-referenced within the text on the basis of studio production stages. The tasks necessary for every production role are divided and arranged at each stage of the production process. The flowchart is divided into the three chronological stages of television studio production: preproduction, production, and postproduction.

This book can be used as a text or reference. The reader can gain a comprehensive understanding of the production process by reading the entire book. The reader also can check specific personnel responsibilities or use particular forms.

Chapter 1 presents flowcharts for preproduction, production, and postproduction stages by personnel role and in sequential task order (see figure).

Chapter 2 details each production task in the order in which it is to be completed.

Chapter 3 provides production organizing forms.

Chapter 4 is a key to terms and information for the production forms in Chapter 3.

Following is a listing of the personnel abbreviations used throughout this text.

Personnel	Abbreviation
Producer	P
Director	D
Talent/host(ess)/moderator	T
Assistant director	AD
Floor director	F
Technical director	TD
Camera operators	CO
Audio director	A
Lighting director	LD
Production assistant	PA
Teleprompter operator	TO
Telecine operator	TC
Videotape recorder operator	VTRO
Video engineer	VEG

Choose a television studio production stage. Here, the PREPRODUCTION stage was chosen.

Each television studio production role is abbreviated (e.g., P) and sequential production tasks numbered (e.g., (1), (2), (3), etc.). To locate the third PREPRODUCTION task responsibility of a PRODUCER (P) look down the checklist for (3).

Every television studio production role and task is listed here and is explained in detail in Chapter 2. The page number after the entry directs you to the explanation. Chapter 2 will also aid you in learning the responsibilities of the other crew members.

This part of the flowchart indicates if there is a production organizing form available in Chapter 3 to assist you in a particular task.

Each television studio production organizing form is explained in detail in a glossary of terms and information required for the form in Chapter 4.

PREPRODUCTION

PRODUCER (P)

☐ (1) Creates/develops a concept for a talk show/entertainment program 9
☐ (2) Begins a proposal to a television station, cable system, public affairs organization (program proposal form) 10
☐ (3) Writes a treatment for the program concept (program treatment form) 10
☐ (4) Develops a program budget (production budget form) 10
☐ (5) Designs a program format (program format form) 10
☐ (6) Creates program titling and opening design (titling/opening design form) 10
☐ (7) Creates a program set design; chooses set properties; authorizes construction (program set design form/studio set properties list form) 11
☐ (8) Writes a preproduction script (preproduction script form) 11
☐ (9) Designs visual graphic requirements (graphic design request form) 11
☐ (10) Secures/maintains studio production facility schedule/relationship (facility request form) 11

Annotated flowchart.

x

Chapter 1

Television Studio Talk Show and Entertainment Program Production

INTRODUCTION

Those television network affiliates or independent television stations that engage in local origination programming most likely will produce some form of local origination programming other than news and in-house commercial production. Public access channels on most cable systems consist primarily of locally produced talk show programs.

Local origination programming can take the form of the talk show or entertainment format. Entertainment programs may be similar to game shows such as "Let's Play Charades" and "Bowling for Dollars," to educational programs such as "It's Academic," and to children's programs like "Bozo the Clown."

One category of local origination programming is public service programming. Public service programming focuses on programs with such talk show formats as the general interest programs like "Community Affairs," age interest programs like "Senior Service," and minority interest programs like "The Black Alternative," to myriad religious programs from the celebration of a Roman Catholic liturgy to a series on Bible teaching.

If a poll were taken of the most common television program format used for studio training in broadcast education, the talk show/entertainment format would probably rate highest. This format lends itself to any studio facility, a minimum production crew, a simple format, and few talent. In addition, the talk show/entertainment format is a popular format, permitting the producer a broad range of topics, a fair amount of audience interest, and local television station marketability. Cable systems thrive on the talk show/entertainment format on their local origination channels.

FLOWCHART AND CHECKLIST

This chapter presents in flowchart and checklist fashion the procedure of the preproduction, production, and postproduction stages of the television production of the talk show/entertainment program. In this flowchart, the procedure is ordered by definition of personnel role responsibility at the preproduction, production, and postproduction stages. Before each entry in the procedure, a checklist box permits the notation of completion of each step as preproduction, production, and postproduction proceeds.

In Chapter 2, the procedure is ordered chronologically by preproduction, production, and postproduction stage task accomplishment.

FLOWCHART AND CHECKLIST FOR STUDIO TALK SHOW AND ENTERTAINMENT PRODUCTION

PRODUCER (P)

	PREPRODUCTION	PRODUCTION	POSTPRODUCTION
	(1) Creates/develops a concept for a talk show/entertainment program **9**	(1) Supervises crew/talent calls; meets with director and talent/crew **25**	(If the talk show/entertainment program is tape delayed, some postproduction may be undertaken. If so, the producer may be involved.)
	(2) Begins a proposal to a television station, cable system, public affairs organization (program proposal form) **10**	(2) Distributes format/rundown sheet for program unit (format/rundown sheet form) **25**	(1) Assumes the decision-making role to add or redo elements of the program **40**
	(3) Writes a treatment for the program concept (program treatment form) **10**	(3) Distributes film sources, prompter script, updated character generator copy, B-roll videotape **26**	(2) Communicates those elements of either the producing stage or the production stage of the program that will become a part of the postproduction process **40**
	(4) Develops a program budget (production budget form) **10**	(4) Handles studio/set arrangements **27**	(3) Continues as in the production stage of the program **40**
	(5) Designs a program format (program format form) **10**	(5) Meets with guest(s) scheduled for program unit **27**	
	(6) Creates program titling and opening design (titling/opening design form) **10**	(6) Handles crew/talent/guest(s) details **27**	
	(7) Creates a program set design; chooses set properties; authorizes construction (program set design form/studio set properties list form) **11**	(7) Monitors the program from the control room **32**	
	(8) Writes a preproduction script (preproduction script form) **11**	(8) Confers with director; makes content/format decisions **36**	
	(9) Designs visual graphic requirements (graphic design request form) **11**	(9) Secures talent release signature(s) **38**	
	(10) Secures/maintains studio production facility schedule/relationship (facility request form) **11**	(10) Calls/meets with director/talent for program critique session **38**	
	(11) Accepts/chooses/hires/meets with program director and studio crew **11**	(11) Calls/meets with director/crew for critique/production session **38**	
	(12) Auditions/chooses/meets talent (talent audition form) **12**		
	(13) Designs/creates future program units: guests, policy, etc. (guest biographical information form; guest booking form) **13**		
	(14) Approves audio/lighting plots; authorizes expenses/purchase requisitions **16**		
	(15) Designs character generator/credits copy (character generator copy form) **16**		
	(16) Obtains copyright/royalty clearances **17**		
	(17) Produces/oversees resources for rehearsal(s): prompter script, B-roll video, film sources, character generator copy, talent wardrobe, make-up **21**		
	(18) Supervises/critiques rehearsal(s) **21**		
	(19) Designs program promotions **23**		

DIRECTOR (D)

	PREPRODUCTION	PRODUCTION	POSTPRODUCTION
	(1) Meets with the producer; meets with production crew **11**	(1) Holds scheduled crew call with crew/talent; receives format/rundown sheet for program unit **25**	(If the talk show/entertainment program is tape delayed, some postproduction may be undertaken. If so, the director may be involved.)
	(2) Studies preproduction documents: proposal, program format, preproduction script, set design **13**	(2) Reviews format/rundown sheet for changes/updates **25**	(1) Assumes responsibility and decision-making role to add or redo elements of the program that involve studio production errors or problems; communicates with producer **40**
	(3) Meets with new talent **13**	(3) Supervises final studio/set arrangement **26**	(2) Alerts specific crew who will be involved in postproduction **40**
	(4) Does a camera blocking plot (camera blocking plot form) **14**	(4) Supervises equipment set-ups/placements **27**	(3) Continues as in the production stage of the program **40**
	(5) Makes studio camera shot lists; distributes shot lists to camera operators (camera shot list form) **16**	(5) Retires to the control room **32**	
	(6) Approves audio/lighting plots **16**	(6) Orients to assigned video source monitors **32**	
	(7) Oversees set construction **16**	(7) Checks intercom connections/response stations **32**	
	(8) Holds a production meeting with studio production crew **18**	(8) Awaits a "ready" cue from production personnel (director's checklist form) **34**	
	(9) Reviews completed set/lighting design **21**	(9) Calls stand-by cue to studio, control room, master control personnel **34**	
		(10) Calls to the videotape recorder operator a "ready to roll tape"; cues to "roll videotape" **34**	

Note: Numbers in boldface type following each item indicate the page number on which the description is located.

□□ (10) Holds/critiques studio rehearsal(s) 21
□□ (11) Sets crew call requirements 23

(11) Awaits timer; counts down to videotape; readies videotape recording; rolls videotape 34
(12) Directs the format/rundown sheet; takes formatted video/audio sources 35
(13) Readies shots/calls "takes" to technical director 35
(14) Confers with producer on production content/format decisions 36
(15) Closes program; stops tape 36
(16) Announces intentions: postproduction, program wrap, studio strike 36
(17) Calls/meets with producer/talent for program critique session 38
(18) Calls/holds critique session with production crew; calls production meeting, if necessary 38

(If the talk show/entertainment program is tape delayed, some postproduction may be undertaken. If so, the talent may be involved.)
□ (1) Readies for those elements of the production that involve the talent in postproduction 41
□ (2) Continues as in the production stage of the program 41

TALENT/HOST(ESS)/MODERATOR (T)

□ (1) Attends audition (talent audition form) 13
□ (2) Is approved as talent; meets with producer/director 13
□ (3) Studies format/preproduction script 13
□ (4) Attends production meeting 18
□ (5) Tries on make-up; tests make-up under lights on-camera 21
□ (6) Decides wardrobe with producer 21
□ (7) Attends/performs rehearsal(s); receives criticism 22

□ (1) Meets with producer/director for crew call; receives format/rundown sheet for program unit 25
□ (2) Reviews format/rundown sheet for changes/updates affecting talent 27
□ (3) Secures talent copy of script from producer 27
□ (4) Reads script for familiarity/pronunciation problems 28
□ (5) Marks script for interpretation 28
□ (6) Meets guests/audience 30
□ (7) Gets dressed; applies make-up 32
□ (8) Reports to the studio set; maintains spike marks 33
□ (9) Checks prompter monitors for reading ease/light reflections 33
□ (10) Assists with the microphone level check 33
□ (11) Has floor director check make-up under set lighting 33
□ (12) Alerts floor director when ready 33
□ (13) Stands by with floor director's call 34
□ (14) Begins with floor director's signal from director to begin; tally light goes on 35
□ (15) Follows format/rundown sheet for program unit for production 36
□ (16) Follows the floor director's communication during production 36
□ (17) Repairs/has repaired make-up during commercial breaks 36
□ (18) Holds studio position pending the director's decision to do postproduction involving the studio talent, program wrap, studio strike call 37
□ (19) Meets with producer/director for critique session 38

ASSISTANT DIRECTOR (AD)

□ (1) Meets with director 12
□ (2) Studies program format/preproduction script 16
□ (3) Attends production meeting 18
□ (4) Assists director 18
□ (5) Works rehearsal(s); attends critique session(s) 22

□ (1) Meets with producer/director for crew call; receives format/rundown sheet for program unit 25
□ (2) Reviews format/rundown sheet for changes/updates; prepares to assist the director 26
□ (3) Orients to video source monitors 32
□ (4) Checks intercom network connections 32
□ (5) Prepares/assists director with format/rundown and crew readiness 32
□ (6) Reviews character generator copy with production assistant 32
□ (7) Resets countdown timer; checks stop watches 33
□ (8) Prepares to follow format/rundown for/with director; notes changes 34
□ (9) Reads clock; times countdowns to opening and other time cues 34

(If the talk show/entertainment program is tape delayed, some postproduction may be undertaken. If so, the assistant director may be involved.)
□ (1) Readies those crew members who may be involved in postproduction work on the program 40
□ (2) Continues as in the production stage of the program 40

PREPRODUCTION	PRODUCTION	POSTPRODUCTION
	☐ (10) Operates/advances remote telecine operation **35**	(If the talk show/entertainment program is tape delayed, some postproduction may be undertaken. If so, the floor director may be involved.)
	☐ (11) Reads expected out-cues to B-roll video/audio sources **35**	☐ (1) Prepares to ready those elements of the production that involve the studio and studio personnel for postproduction **40**
	☐ (12) Keeps tabs on/times prerecorded video/audio sources **35**	☐ (2) Continues as in the production stage of the program **40**
	☐ (13) Operates videotape playback decks by remote control; readies videotape playback source(s) for operation **35**	
	☐ (14) Readies character generator screen copy **35**	
	☐ (15) Prepares any postproduction needs from the production crew; assists with program wrap/studio strike **37**	
	☐ (16) Oversees studio strike in control room **37**	
	☐ (17) Meets with producer/director for critique/production meeting **38**	

FLOOR DIRECTOR (F)

PREPRODUCTION	PRODUCTION	POSTPRODUCTION
☐ (1) Meets with the director **12**	☐ (1) Meets with producer/director for crew call; receives format/rundown sheet for program unit **25**	
☐ (2) Studies the program format **15**	☐ (2) Reviews format/rundown sheet for studio expectations, order of program, changes/updates **26**	
☐ (3) Attends production meeting **18**	☐ (3) Assumes responsibility for studio/set/talent/crew during studio use **27**	
☐ (4) Works rehearsal(s); attends critique session(s) **22**	☐ (4) Organizes studio set for readiness; checks props on spike marks **32**	
	☐ (5) Checks/calls talent/guest(s); monitors readiness **33**	
	☐ (6) Checks intercom network connections **33**	
	☐ (7) Checks camera operators; monitors readiness **33**	
	☐ (8) Checks lighting/light pattern working order **33**	
	☐ (9) Checks audio foldback in studio **33**	
	☐ (10) Makes make-up check on talent/guests; adds powder, as necessary **33**	
	☐ (11) Alerts director to studio readiness **33**	
	☐ (12) Communicates the director's commands to studio personnel **34**	
	☐ (13) Calls/maintains readiness in the studio **34**	
	☐ (14) Repeats all countdowns to the studio to a 2-second call **34**	
	☐ (15) Signals to the talent which camera is "on" **35**	
	☐ (16) Maintains communication between director and studio **35**	
	☐ (17) Communicates to talent during commercial breaks **35**	
	☐ (18) Repairs talent make-up during commercial breaks **36**	
	☐ (19) Communicates to the director any information from the studio **36**	
	☐ (20) Relays the director's call for a hold in studio positions pending a call for postproduction, program wrap, studio strike **37**	
	☐ (21) Oversees complete strike of the studio **37**	
	☐ (22) Meets with producer/director for critique/production meeting **38**	

TECHNICAL DIRECTOR (TD)

PREPRODUCTION	PRODUCTION	POSTPRODUCTION
☐ (1) Meets with the director **12**	☐ (1) Meets with producer/director for crew call; receives format/rundown sheet for program unit **26**	(If the talk show/entertainment program is tape delayed, some postproduction may be undertaken. If so, the technical director may be involved.)
☐ (2) Familiarizes self with format/preproduction script **16**	☐ (2) Reviews format/rundown sheet for changes/updates **26**	☐ (1) Prepares to add or redo those elements of the program in postproduction that involve the switches **40**
☐ (3) Attends production meeting **18**	☐ (3) Checks intercom network connections **31**	☐ (2) Communicates to the video recording operator what video sources will be involved in postproduction **40**
☐ (4) Works rehearsal(s); attends critique session(s) **22**	☐ (4) Checks with videotape recorder operator for B-roll source playback; routes assigned signal through switcher **31**	☐ (3) Continues as in the production stage of the program **40**
	☐ (5) Sets up the switcher for required effects; tests effects **31**	
	☐ (6) Sets video levels with technical director **31**	

CAMERA OPERATORS (CO)

- (1) Meet with director **12**
- (2) Work program format and shot lists **16**
- (3) Attend production meeting **18**
- (4) Study camera placement **18**
- (5) Attend rehearsal(s)/critique session(s) **22**

- (1) Meet with producer/director at crew call; receive format/rundown sheet for program unit **25**
- (2) Review format/rundown sheet for changes/updates **26**
- (3) Set up/prepare assigned camera and placement **28**
- (4) Review/attach shot list to camera **29**
- (5) Check cameras for zoom, pan, tilt, dolly, truck, pedestal, arc control **31**
- (6) Secure adequate camera cable behind camera for movement flexibility **31**
- (7) Check intercom connections; announce readiness **31**
- (8) Practice required shots of set/talent **31**
- (9) Check lens filter choice **32**
- (10) Maintain depth of field focus during/after changes in camera position **32**
- (11) Set opening shots; alert floor director when ready **32**
- (12) Maintain ready positions until director calls for a new set-up **35**
- (13) Listen/follow the director's calls **36**
- (14) Hold studio positions pending a decision to do studio postproduction work, program wrap, studio strike call **37**
- (15) Meet with producer/director for critique/production meeting **38**

- (7) Alerts director when ready **31**
- (8) Listens/responds to the director's commands **34**
- (9) Switches appropriate video sources **34**
- (10) Prepares for any postproduction; stops down switcher at call for a wrap **37**
- (11) Shuts down switcher with wrap/studio strike call **37**
- (12) Meets with producer/director for critique/production meeting **38**

(If the talk show/entertainment program is tape delayed, some postproduction may be undertaken. If so, the studio cameras may be involved.)
- ☐ (1) Prepare to ready those elements of the production that involve the studio cameras for postproduction **40**
- ☐ (2) Continue as in the production stage of the program **40**

AUDIO DIRECTOR (A)

- (1) Meets with the director **12**
- (2) Studies the program format, preproduction script, set design **15**
- (3) Designs audio/microphone plots (audio plot form) **15**
- (4) Lists sound effects/music needs (sound effects/music plot form) **16**
- (5) Submits the audio plot/effects needs to the producer and director for approval **16**
- (6) Attends production meeting **18**
- (7) Attends rehearsal(s)/critique session(s) **22**

- (1) Meets with producer/director at crew call; receives format/rundown sheet for program unit **25**
- (2) Reviews format/rundown sheet for studio microphone needs, prerecorded audio needs, playback needs, changes/updates **26**
- (3) Begins studio audio equipment set-up **27**
- (4) Runs microphone cables; records studio microphone inputs **28**
- (5) Patches inputs into audio control board in control room **28**
- (6) Sets levels for playback audio cartridge sources **32**
- (7) Checks and re-cues prerecorded audio sources **32**
- (8) Checks network intercom connections **32**
- (9) Patches/tests audio foldback sound to the studio **33**
- (10) Calls for studio talent microphone check; sets levels **33**
- (11) Sets audio levels for B-roll playback video source(s) **33**
- (12) Alerts director when ready **33**
- (13) Awaits director's opening cues **34**
- (14) Follows director's calls during program production **35**
- (15) Prepares for postproduction: closes down control board with wrap/studio strike call by director **37**
- (16) Meets with producer/director for critique/production meeting **38**

(If the talk show/entertainment program is tape delayed, some postproduction may be undertaken. If so, the audio director may be involved.)
- ☐ (1) Prepares to ready those elements of the production that involve audio sources for postproduction **40**
- ☐ (2) Continues as in the production stage of the program **40**

	PREPRODUCTION	PRODUCTION	POSTPRODUCTION

LIGHTING DIRECTOR (LD)

PREPRODUCTION	PRODUCTION	POSTPRODUCTION
(1) Meets with the director 12	(1) Meets with producer/director at crew call; receives format/rundown sheet for program unit 26	(If the talk show/entertainment program is tape delayed, some postproduction may be undertaken. If so, the lighting director may be involved.)
(2) Works the studio set design/property list 15	(2) Reviews format/rundown sheet for changes/updates 28	☐ (1) Readies those lighting elements of the production that involve the lighting director in postproduction 41
(3) Designs lighting plot (set lighting plot form) 16	(3) Checks lighting pattern/light instruments on set 28	☐ (2) Continues as in the production stage of the program 41
(4) Submits lighting plot to the producer and director for approval 16	(4) Checks lighting effects over control room monitors 29	
(5) Attends production meeting 18	(5) Checks for unwanted reflections 29	
(6) Lights the completed set 19	(6) Makes lighting intensity/light instrument changes 29	
(7) Reviews the studio set light pattern with the director 20	(7) Alerts director when ready 29	
(8) Attends rehearsal(s)/critique session(s) 22	(8) Listens for director's call for lighting cues/changes 34	
(9) Makes lighting adjustments 23	(9) Monitors set/talent lighting over control room monitors during videotaping 35	
	(10) Prepares for postproduction: strikes floor lights; turns off set lights at director's program wrap/studio strike call 37	
	(11) Meets with producer/director for critique/production meeting 39	

PRODUCTION ASSISTANT (PA)

PREPRODUCTION	PRODUCTION	POSTPRODUCTION
(1) Meets with director 12	(1) Meets with producer/director for crew call; receives format/rundown sheet for program unit 26	(If the talk show/entertainment program is tape delayed, some postproduction may be undertaken.) The production assistant may be involved.)
(2) Secures character generator text copy form from producer 17	(2) Reviews format/rundown sheet for changes/updates 26	☐ (1) Prepares to ready those elements of the production that involve the character generator for postproduction 40
(3) Attends production meeting 19	(3) Secures character generator copy from producer 29	☐ (2) Continues as in the production stage of the program 40
(4) Enters character generator copy (character generator copy form) 19	(4) Enters/records in character generator 29	
(5) Works rehearsal(s); attends critique session(s) 23	(5) Checks intercom network connections 29	
	(6) Reviews character generator copy with assistant director 32	
	(7) Alerts director when ready 32	
	(8) Changes/maintains relevant information of each screen text for succeeding/current use 34	
	(9) Advances character generator screen copy when technical director clears previous matte from program line 35	
	(10) Prepares for postproduction; turns character generator off with wrap/studio strike call 37	
	(11) Meets with producer/director for critique/production meeting 39	

If talent will require studio prompter copy:

TELEPROMPTER OPERATOR (TO)

PREPRODUCTION	PRODUCTION	POSTPRODUCTION
(1) Meets with director 12	(1) Meets with producer/director for crew call; receives format/rundown sheet 26	(If the talk show/entertainment program is tape delayed, some postproduction may be undertaken. If so, the teleprompter operator may be involved.)
(2) Reviews program format/rundown sheet for order of program elements 17	(2) Reviews program format/rundown sheet for order of program elements/updates 29	☐ (1) Prepares to ready those elements of the production that involve the teleprompter for postproduction 40
(3) Attends production meeting 19	(3) Secures teleprompter script copy from producer 30	☐ (2) Continues as in the production stage of the program 41
(4) Sets up teleprompter bed 19	(4) Prepares script copy for teleprompter bed 30	
(5) Secures teleprompter script copy from producer 19	(5) Checks video reproduction of script at camera monitors 30	
(6) Prepares to run script copy for camera monitor test 19	(6) Permits talent to check reading pleasure and to practice with script; checks foldback sound in studio 30	
(7) Works rehearsal(s); attends critique session(s) 23	(7) Alerts floor director when ready 30	
	(8) Waits for the floor director's opening cue to begin 34	
	(9) Follows talent carefully; keeps script copy at desired screen height 35	
	(10) Holds studio position; prepares for postproduction, program wrap, studio strike 37	
	(11) Meets with producer/director for critique/production meeting 39	

If 35mm slides or 16mm film will be used:

TELECINE OPERATOR (TC)

☐ (1) Meets with director 12
☐ (2) Reviews/studies format/rundown sheet 17
☐ (3) Attends production meeting 19
☐ (4) Secures film sources from producer and/or graphic artist 19
☐ (5) Works rehearsal(s); attends critique session(s) 23

☐ (1) Meets with producer/director for crew call; receives format/rundown sheet 26
☐ (2) Reviews format/rundown sheet for program unit and graphic list for program order/changes/updates 26
☐ (3) Secures any film sources from producer 30
☐ (4) Loads telecine with slides/film, as necessary 30
☐ (5) Checks telecine operation/order of film sources 30
☐ (6) Checks intercom network connections 30
☐ (7) Communicates to assistant director when ready 31
☐ (8) Operates/advances telecine during program; switches remote control to assistant director in control room 35
☐ (9) Stands by for changes/correction during program; reloads sources 36
☐ (10) Holds telecine operation; prepares for postproduction; strikes film sources with director's call for a wrap 37
☐ (11) Meets with producer/director for critique/production meeting 39

(If the talk show/entertainment program is tape delayed, some postproduction may be undertaken. If so, the telecine operator may be involved.)
☐ (1) Prepares to ready those elements of the production that involve the telecine and film sources in postproduction 41
☐ (2) Continues as in the production stage of the program 41

VIDEOTAPE RECORDER OPERATOR (VTRO)

☐ (1) Meets with director 12
☐ (2) Determines required record/playback deck needs from format/rundown sheet 19
☐ (3) Checks operation of video recorders/playback units 19
☐ (4) Performs preventive maintenance 19
☐ (5) Attends production meeting 19
☐ (6) Secures videotapes for A-roll and B-roll from producer 19
☐ (7) Chooses playback and record videotape decks 19
☐ (8) Determines videotape stock needs (source tapes, master tape(s)) 19
☐ (9) Works rehearsal(s); attends critique session(s) 23

☐ (1) Meets with producer/director for crew call; receives format/rundown sheet for program unit 26
☐ (2) Reviews format/rundown sheet for videotape playback/recording needs/changes/updates 26
☐ (3) Secures any B-roll videotape from producer 31
☐ (4) Chooses/prepares record/playback videotape deck; selects videotape recording stock; threads decks; cues up playback machines for B-roll videotape 31
☐ (5) Checks intercom network connections 31
☐ (6) Alerts technical director of record/playback deck choices 31
☐ (7) Sets video levels of videotape sources with technical director 31
☐ (8) Switches remote control of playback videotape recorder to the control room/assistant director 31
☐ (9) Alerts director when ready 31
☐ (10) Responds to the director's call to ready videotape/roll videotape; begins videotape recorder operation 34
☐ (11) Monitors playback/recording videotape machines 36
☐ (12) Prepares for postproduction needs; strikes videotape recording with director's call for program wrap/studio strike 37
☐ (13) Rewinds videotapes; labels videotape storage case 38
☐ (14) Meets with producer/director for critique/production meeting 39

(If the talk show/entertainment program is tape delayed, some postproduction may be undertaken. If so, the videotape recorder operator may be involved.)
☐ (1) Readies those video recording elements of the production that involve the videotape recorder operator 41
☐ (2) Continues as in the production stage of the program 41

VIDEO ENGINEER (VEG)

☐ (1) Checks cameras with camera operators 19
☐ (2) Does preventive maintenance 19
☐ (3) Checks teleprompter monitors on cameras 19
☐ (4) Uncaps cameras 19
☐ (5) Sets video levels/lenses with studio lights 19
☐ (6) Routes external signal to camera monitors for camera operator use 20
☐ (7) Checks tally light operation on cameras 20
☐ (8) Works rehearsal(s)/attends critique session(s) 23

☐ (1) Meets with producer/director for crew call; receives format/rundown sheet for program unit 26
☐ (2) Reviews format/rundown sheet for changes/updates 28
☐ (3) Readies studio cameras for videotaping/shading 28
☐ (4) Checks video levels of cameras with lighting on set 29
☐ (5) Alerts director when cameras are ready 29
☐ (6) Monitors video level of cameras during program taping 36
☐ (7) Alerts director to soft focused cameras during videotaping 36
☐ (8) Prepares for postproduction needs; caps cameras with director's call for a program wrap/studio strike 37
☐ (9) Meets with producer/director for critique/production meeting 39

(If the talk show/entertainment program is tape delayed, some postproduction may be undertaken. If so, the video engineer may be involved.)
☐ (1) Readies those video production elements of the program that involve video engineering in postproduction 41
☐ (2) Continues as in the production stage of the program 41

Chapter 2

Processes of Television Studio Talk Show and Entertainment Program Production

INTRODUCTION

Successful talk show/entertainment programs can distinguish themselves, as do most other television formats, on quality preproduction, a detail-conscious and thorough producer, and a good talent (moderator, host, or hostess). This chapter is devoted to fostering thorough quality preproduction. The talk show/entertainment program can be adapted to any facility, any crew, or any format. Broadcast education, cable systems, and network affiliates will all benefit from the stages and process of talk show/entertainment program development.

THE PREPRODUCTION PROCESS

• Personnel

As stated in the Preface, the production of television entertainment programming is one of the simplest productions in the multiple camera studio genre of television programming. The process is quite simple, and it involves a minimum studio production crew. Above-the-line staff may include an executive producer, but generally requires only a producer. In this genre of television programming, a producer is responsible for more than the producer in most other programming genres. A minimum production crew includes a director, an assistant director, a technical director, an audio director, a floor director, a production assistant, a telecine operator (if film sources will be needed), and three camera operators. A lighting director, video engineer, and videotape recorder operator round out the crew. A studio prompter operator may be required if studio script copy will need to be read by talent, but this role would be optional.

Producer (P) The producer begins the process of talk show/entertainment program preproduction. The producer may be a staff member of the television station or cable system or a freelance agent for a public affairs organization. A principal role for a producer, especially a freelance producer, is creating the concept for the program and writing the program proposal. For a television station, a cable system, or a public affairs organization, the preproduction responsibilities for the producer also include creating a format, studio set, preproduction script, and titling; keeping the budget; choosing a director and crew; and handling most details from obtaining copyright clearances to creating titling and graphics for the program. The qualities of a producer include being able to create ideas, having organizational abilities, paying attention to detail, and being thorough in each task.

Director (D) The director plays a strong production role, but has preproduction responsibilities as well. All details of studio production preparation fall to the director. Almost all creative and artistic production elements of the program are the responsibility of the director. The qualities of a director include experience with directing talent and crew and knowledge of the television studio production process.

Camera operators (CO) The studio camera operators have minimum but important preproduction responsibilities. They must work with the program format and their camera shot lists.

Lighting director (LD) The lighting director's preproduction responsibilities are creative—designing the lighting—and technical—producing the lighting design with the studio light instruments.

Audio director (A) The audio director has preproduction responsibilities ranging from the aesthetic—designing the audio plot, music, and sound effects—to the technical—physically placing cable runs and microphones for studio production.

Assistant director (AD) The assistant director works closely with the director and has a minimum of preproduction responsibilities.

Floor director (F) The floor director's responsibilities are limited to general studio preparation and to studying the format.

Technical director (TD) The technical director's preproduction responsibilities rest in knowing what visual techniques and special effects may be required from the production switcher for the program.

Videotape recorder operator (VTRO) The videotape recorder operator has the preproduction responsibility to determine the videotape stock necessary for the production.

Video engineer (VEG) The video engineer, while not a part of the immediate production crew, is nonetheless a part of the studio crew during preproduction preparation.

Production assistant (PA) The production assistant's primary preproduction responsibility is to prepare all character generator copy for the program's production—slate, titling, and any other screen text required.

Talent (T) Talent for the program may involve a host, hostess, or moderator (master/mistress of ceremonies). The talent's preproduction responsibilities involve becoming familiar with the program format and the talent's role definition within that format.

• **Preproduction Stages**

Creating and developing a concept for a talk show/ entertainment program (P 1) The producer is the catalyst for creating a new program idea. The producer is either a staff person at a television station or cable system or a freelancer who might work for a public service organization wishing to sponsor a new television program. A freelancer could develop a new program concept and market the idea to the television station without any sponsorship. In either case, an idea for a new program normally begins with a producer.

FIGURE 2–1
Personnel organization chart. This chart attempts to organize all talk show/entertainment production personnel into levels of responsibility.

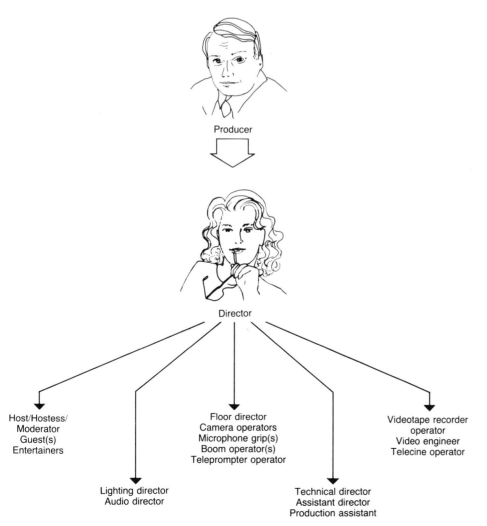

Producer

Director

Host/Hostess/
Moderator
Guest(s)
Entertainers

Lighting director
Audio director

Floor director
Camera operators
Microphone grip(s)
Boom operator(s)
Teleprompter operator

Technical director
Assistant director
Production assistant

Videotape recorder
operator
Video engineer
Telecine operator

FIGURE 2–2
The talk show/entertainment program producer. Most talk show/entertainment programs begin with a producer's idea. A program idea is passed before people who can sponsor or produce it.

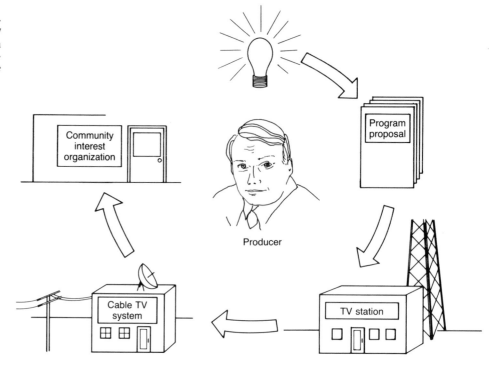

Beginning a proposal to a television station, cable system, or public service organization (P 2)   After the concept or idea for a new television program is created, the producer writes a proposal. The proposal is submitted to the management of a television station, a cable system operator, or the board of directors of a public service organization for the purpose of suggesting and designing a new television program. The proposal for a television program should contain at least a treatment and a budget for the new program. Additional documents might consist of a preproduction script, a set design, and a proposed program format. The proposal might also contain a videotape pilot of the program. A *pilot* is a videotaped edition of the new program idea. (See the program proposal form.)

Writing a treatment for the program concept (P 3)
The first step in creating a proposal for a new program idea is to write a treatment. The treatment contains a description of the proposed program, which includes the goals and objectives to be achieved by the new program and an analysis of the target audience.

Once the target audience is identified, a producer chooses the video and audio production values that might be used in the production of the program to attract and hook that audience. *Production values* are those video images and audio techniques in television that tend to attract the attention and interest of the audience; e.g., fifties music might attract a middle-aged audience, and fad fashions and strobe light images might attract teenagers.

From the goals and objectives and audience elements in the treatment, the producer writes a production statement—a short verbal statement that captures the specific goal and objective of the production—that can be used as

a verbal motivator during all stages of the production. For example, a production statement for a senior citizen television program, "Growing New," might be "Age, wisdom, and experience spell life." The production statement is then used in any way that keeps the crew's attention focused on the goals or objectives of the program during preproduction; e.g., printing it on the slate or on the format/rundown sheet. It is hoped that all creative and production decisions made for the program will be based on the stated goals and objectives. (See the program treatment form.)

Developing a program budget (P 4)   The producer develops a proposed budget for the program. The budget often means the difference between the success or failure of a new program. A producer should be as accurate in cost estimation as possible. A model production budget form directs the producer to consider line items that may not be thought of otherwise. (See the production budget form.)

Designing a program format (P 5)   The producer includes a program format in the program proposal. While it may not be required in a proposal, the information eventually will be required. The program format is a graphic representation of the proposed program in terms of program segments designed for the time slot of the program. A format also includes commercial break segments. The completed format for a program unit becomes the studio production format/rundown sheet. (See the program format form.)

Creating the program titling and opening design (P 6)
Another preproduction step in creating a new program is the design of the titling for the new program and the opening sequence of images or camera shots. The producer

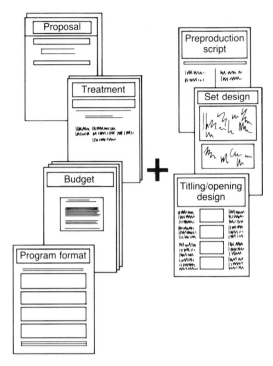

FIGURE 2–3
Elements of a program proposal. A proposal statement, program treatment, budget, and program format are important to a program proposal. Optional elements include a preproduction script, a set design, and titling/opening design ideas.

designs and chooses the type style and size for the title of the program. Type style is a way to set the image of the program and is an important step in new program design. The design for the opening of the program includes choosing the sequence of video screens, images, or camera shots that set the stage and convey the concept for the program to the audience. With computerized images and graphics in use today, some form of moving images and titling may be chosen. Stylized images may be designed. However, the simple program opening of presenting the talent in place on the studio set invites the audience immediately into the program with little extraneous distraction. Any opening might be used when properly motivated. Each choice should have its rationale. (See the titling/opening design form.)

Creating a program set design, choosing set properties, and authorizing construction (P 7) The producer is responsible for beginning a set design. The set design is another optional document to include in the program proposal. The producer may choose to do the design or hire a consultant or outside designer. A sketch of the proposed set goes a long way to express the concept of a new program. Part of designing a set is providing a list of properties that will be required as part of the set design. These properties include furniture and set appointments, such as plants, statues, and books. (See the program set design form and the studio set properties list form.)

Writing a preproduction script (P 8) The producer writes a preproduction script for the proposed program.

A preproduction script for a new program is a television script containing announcer's copy and/or talent opening copy. The announcer's copy would tell the audience, for example, how to get on the program as part of a studio audience, how to suggest topics for future programs, and how to ask questions of guests. Such information as mailing address and telephone number are part of a preproduction script. The preproduction script is not an attempt to script a live program but only to record prerecorded copy or standard opening or closing and commercial break tosses. Suggested music or other sound effects should also be included in the preproduction script. (See the preproduction script form.)

Designing visual graphic requirements for the program (P 9) The producer designs any visual graphic requirements for the new program. Graphic requirements can be as simple as a full screen envelope with the mailing address of the program on the front for audience correspondence. The screen text giving a disclaimer or telephone number is an example of preproduction graphic design. (See the graphic design request form.)

Securing a studio production facility, agreeing on a studio production schedule, and maintaining the relationship (P 10) The producer is responsible for the production studio facility for the new program. When developing the budget, the producer needs some idea of studio costs for the proposed program. Contacting a production facility, agreeing on a production schedule, and maintaining the relationship with the facility during preproduction are the responsibilities of the producer. Preproduction studio time must be secured for set construction, set lighting, and program rehearsal(s) before a production videotaping session. Making arrangements for continuing production of future program units is also part of early facility planning and relationship building by the producer. (See the facility request form.)

Accepting, choosing, or hiring a program director and studio production crew and meeting with them (P 11) The producer will know after establishing a relationship with a studio facility whether there is a director available and a full studio crew, or whether the producer can or must put a production crew together. Most studio facilities have staff directors and intact production crews. The producer may have the opportunity to choose among directors for a director for the program. Arrangements should be made for meeting with the director and the production crew after assembling the crew. Communication with the production crew at an early stage will facilitate later rehearsal(s) and program videotapings. The producer should be ready to share copies of such preproduction documents as program format, preproduction script, and set design with the director and and crew.

Meeting with the producer and the production crew (D 1) The director meets with the producer as soon as possible after receiving the appointment to direct the new program. In turn, the director chooses to meet with the entire production crew as a first step to working together. This is not a production meeting in the strict sense, but a relationship building meeting. Assignments and expectations are communicated to the production crew at this meeting. The director should have a set of preproduction documents from the producer to distribute to crew members. These documents could include a copy of the program proposal, the program format, preproduction script, or set design. The more information the director can share with the crew at this meeting the better the remaining preproduction tasks can flow.

The meetings with the director and the production crew can be held individually or as a group. More specific role requirements can be communicated better in individual face-to-face meetings. The production meeting with the entire crew should be held close to the first rehearsal for the new program.

Meeting with the director (AD 1) The assistant director meets with the director as a first step to building a production crew for the new program. At this meeting, the concept of the program is presented and the director defines the assistant director's job requirements.

Meeting with the director (F 1) The floor director meets with the director at the beginning of building a studio production crew. The floor director is given access to the format and set design as an introduction to the floor director's role in the studio during rehearsal(s) and production videotapings.

Meeting with the director (TD 1) The technical director meets with the director and is introduced to the program concept. The director conveys the director's expectations for the picturization of the program that the technical director, through the switcher, will create. *Picturization* is the sequence of video images that the technical director effects through the production switcher during program videotaping. A copy of the format and the producer's title and opening design form would be helpful to the technical director at this stage.

Meeting with the director (CO 1) The camera operators meet with the director as an orientation to their roles during rehearsal(s) and production videotaping. The first meeting is an opportunity to build a working relationship with the director and to discuss the expectations the director has for camera work during the program's production.

Meeting with the director (A 1) The audio director meets with the director as the first opportunity to receive the preproduction documents that will permit the audio director to begin preproduction planning for the program's production. The audio director also receives the scheduled deadline for the audio plot for the program. The audio director needs a copy of the set design and the preproduction script, which will enable him or her to determine the audio requirements for the program's production.

Meeting with the director (LD 1) The lighting director meets with the director as a first step in essential preproduction work for lighting the set. The lighting director receives the set design and the titling/opening design forms. These forms should enable the lighting director to begin a lighting plot for the studio set, which will meet the needs of the production. The lighting director should also receive from the director at this meeting a deadline for submitting the lighting plot for approval as well as a scheduled deadline for the first rehearsal and, therefore, a deadline for having completed the lighting design in the studio.

Meeting with the director (PA 1) The production assistant meets with the director. This gives the production assistant a start on preproduction work that has to be completed before the first program rehearsal. The production assistant has to know how much of the new program's visual look requires the character generator. The titling/opening design form is helpful in providing the necessary information. The preproduction script may also contain an indication of the need for character generator text (e.g., mailing address for correspondence, a telephone number, etc.). It is probably too early into the preproduction of the program to expect character generator copy such as closing credits to be ready.

Meeting with the director (TO 1) If there will be a need for talent to read studio prompter copy during the production of the program, a teleprompter operator meets with the director. This orients the prompter operator to the needs the production will have for copy to be read during the program. If a prompter is available in the studio, it may be used to present and update the program format/rundown sheet to the talent during production videotaping.

Meeting with the director (TC 1) If any film sources (e.g., 35mm or 16mm) will be used in production, a telecine operator may be needed on the studio production crew. The telecine operator meets with the director. It is possible that 35mm slides will be a part of the opening of a talk show/entertainment program or that guests will need slides as part of their presentation. For these reasons, a telecine operator should be part of the crew from the beginning.

Meeting with the director (VTRO 1) The videotape recorder operator also meets with the director. In addition to the videotape recording requirements of the program, videotape B-rolling may be needed. *B-rolling* refers to the process of inserting another videotape source(s) into the primary videotape. The primary videotape is called the *A-roll*. These requirements necessitate the involvement of the videotape recorder operator as early as possible in preproduction. The program format may help the videotape recorder operator determine the videotape record and playback needs.

Auditioning, choosing, and meeting with the talent—host, hostess, or moderator—for the program (P 12) The producer begins the process of finding talent—host, hostess, or moderator—for the new program. This can be accomplished by open auditions or by invitation. Auditions for talent for a program should be done on videotape. Prospective talent should be seen over the screen just as they will on the program. Prospective talent may be asked to perform, deliver copy, or read prompter copy in order to give a producer a sample of on-air appearance, voice, and physical deportment. (See the talent audition form.)

The producer should make a choice of talent based on the audition responses from all of the prospective talent. Because the producer has the initial program concept in mind, the producer is best qualified to make the choice of talent for the program.

Once the host, hostess, or moderator has been chosen, talent should be given the preproduction documents that best orient the talent to the role requirements for the program.

Attending the audition for talent—host, hostess, or moderator (T 1)   Prospective talent for the host, hostess, or moderator position on the program attend the audition for the role. The audition may be advertised publicly or circulated privately. The audition may even be known by invitation only. The talent attend an audition expecting to be videotaped, often in the studio on the set of the program if it is completed by the time of the audition. Talent may have to read prompter copy, perform ad-lib monologue, or improvise. Talent should come to an audition with a résumé—a summary of past public performance work, a black-and-white glossy photograph of him- or herself, and credentials of membership in any performers' union. A minimum of make-up might be worn; black or white clothes should be avoided for a videotape audition. Black tends to absorb too much light and white reflects too much studio light. Each can give a false representation of the best appearance for prospective talent.

Studying the preproduction documents: program proposal, program format, preproduction script, set design, etc. (D 2)   The director takes time to study all of the preproduction documents that the producer has created for the program. These documents, which include the proposal (with treatment and budget), program format, preproduction script, studio set design, etc., should orient the director to the new program. The director will need these documents to prepare for a production meeting with

the crew and to do any remaining preproduction work before the first program rehearsal.

Being approved as talent for the program and meeting with the producer and director (T 2)   The talent chosen meets as soon as possible with both the producer and the director. This meeting should provide an opportunity for orienting the talent to the program and to allow the talent and director to begin to build a relationship. The more easily the talent and director can read each other, the better the control room and studio set relationship will work. At this meeting, preproduction documents should be given to the talent as a primary source of role expectation. Documents such as the program format, preproduction script are critical to helping the talent develop at this stage of preproduction.

Creating and designing future program units and guest policy (P 13)   As the new program moves through preproduction preparation to rehearsal(s) and videotaping, the producer has to create and develop a procedure for screening, scheduling, and clearing guests for future program units. Establishing policy for guest appearances is important even before the program gets on the air. (See the guest biographical information form and the guest booking form.)

Studying program format, preproduction script (T 3)   Once the talent is chosen for the role of host, hostess, or moderator, the talent begins to study the preproduction materials to become informed about the role expectations. The program format and preproduction script are two documents to best introduce talent at this stage to the required role for the program.

Meeting with the chosen talent—host, hostess, or moderator (D 3)   The director meets with the talent to begin building a good relationship between them. The talent needs to learn the role requirements from the view the director has from the control room (where the director works) and the studio set (where the talent performs). The better this relationship, the better the communication between them.

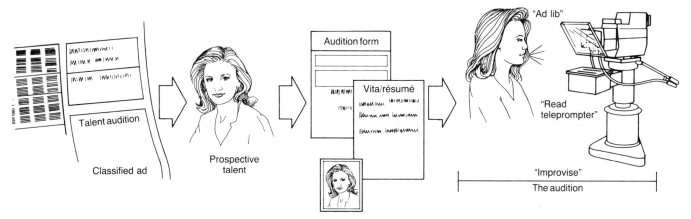

FIGURE 2–4
The talent audition. Classified ads in trade magazines begin the search for talent. Talent apply for an audition with a vita or résumé, a photo of him- or herself, and an application. The audition may require ad-libbing, reading prompter copy, or improvising.

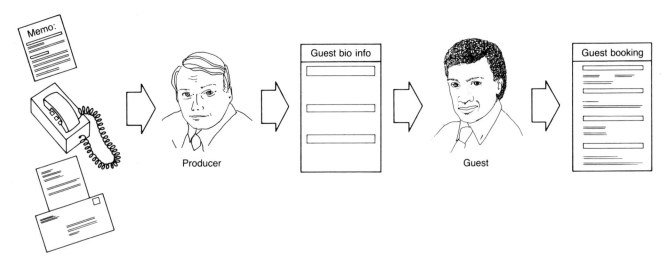

FIGURE 2–5
Setting guest appearances. From ideas and leads for guests for the program, the producer develops screening and information gathering procedures for guests. A guest biographical form is used before deciding on an appearance, and a guest booking form for setting a program date and guest appearance.

Doing a camera blocking plot (D 4) The director begins one of the important preproduction stages by blocking cameras on the set design form. The bird's eye view of the proposed set from the set design form is used for this purpose. The director also has to take the program format and preproduction script and determine the placement of the three cameras. By indicating a cross-camera design, the director defines basic camera shots and lens framing for the cameras to effect the proposed format design for the program. A cross-camera design defines

the roles of the three studio cameras by indicating that camera 1 and camera 3, for example, concentrate their placement and shots in an X fashion; i.e., camera 1 covering camera left (stage right) talent and camera 3 covering camera right (stage left) talent. Camera 2 is usually defined as a safety or cover shot camera, shooting straight on. Camera 2 is framed with a LS (long shot) or XLS (extreme long shot) framing throughout program videotaping. Camera 2 is called a *safety camera* because, by maintaining a shot on the entire set throughout videotap-

FIGURE 2–6
The blocking plot. The director creates a camera blocking plot from a bird's eye view of the set design. Set, properties, talent, and camera movement are blocked.

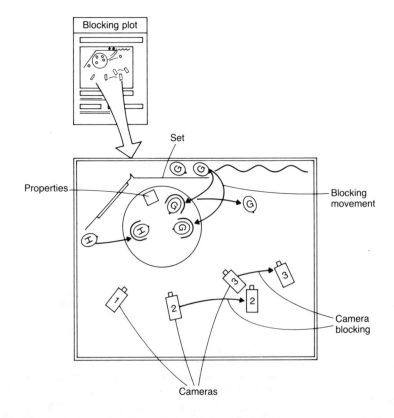

ing, the director always has a shot (hence, a safety shot) that can be depended upon when talent movement or other camera changes inhibit taking either the shot from camera 1 or the shot from camera 3. It is from the camera blocking plot that the director creates the camera shot lists. (See the camera blocking plot form.)

Studying the program format (F 2)   The floor director best prepares for the coming production meeting and rehearsal(s) by studying the program format received during the meeting with the director. This format presents the order of the proposed program and orients the floor director to what will be expected in the studio during videotaping.

Studying the program format, preproduction script, and set design (A 2)   The audio director takes the preproduction documents received from the meeting with the director and begins studying them with an eye to designing the audio plot for the program. The audio director needs to plan sound pickup for the production and also will be responsible for other sound effects for

the program, especially the music. The choice of music may be left to the audio director or may be chosen by the producer. In either case, the audio director will have to alert the producer to any copyright needs and synchronization requirements. The audio director will have to determine what prerecorded tracks (e.g., an announcer's voice-over copy) may have to be completed before rehearsal begins.

Working the studio set design and the property list (LD 2)   The lighting director begins preproduction requirements by studying the set design and property list. These documents orient the lighting director to the studio set elements that have to be lighted for the rehearsal(s) and eventual studio production videotaping.

Designing the audio and microphone plot (A 3)   The audio director designs the audio plot and microphone requirements to pick up program sound for the production. Designing the audio plot requires the set design in order to plan microphone cable runs (placement of properties—i.e., furniture—will indicate the sound pickup

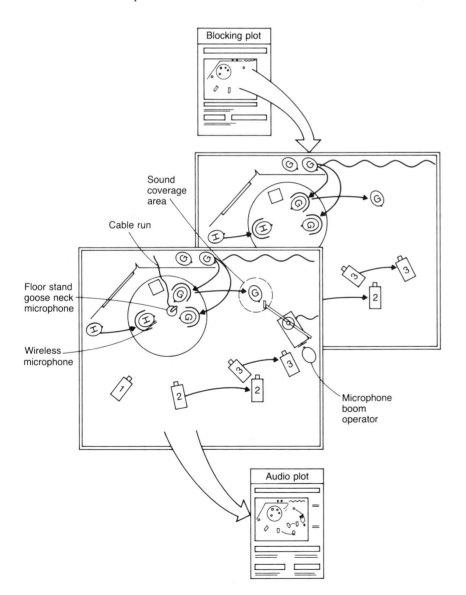

FIGURE 2–7
The audio plot. The audio director creates the audio plot from the director's blocking plot. Microphones, cable runs, and sound coverage areas are indicated.

position of talent or guests) and the camera blocking plot to plan camera placement (to avoid cable crossing). The audio director also has to choose the types of microphones required for the program. Some talk show/entertainment programs use platform boom microphones to avoid putting on and taking off microphones when changing guests during a program. If a platform boom microphone is required, microphone grips and boom operators will be required for the production crew. (See the audio plot form.)

Listing sound effects and music needs (A 4) The audio director lists the sound effects (not necessarily in the more narrow sense of recorded natural sounds, but in the more general sense of electronically produced sounds) and music requirements for the new program, including theme music and prerecorded voice-over tracks. The audio director must inform the producer of copyrighted materials proposed and the need to get clearance and synchronization rights for the music. (See the sound effects/music plot form.)

Submitting the audio plot and sound effects/music needs to the producer and director for approval (A 5) The audio director submits the audio plot and sound effects and music requirements to the producer and the director for approval. This approval is not only a creative approval to the effects and music chosen but also the authorization to make the necessary purchases to acquire the requested effects and/or music.

Designing the lighting plot for the studio set (LD 3) After studying the set design, the camera blocking plot, and the titling/opening design form, the lighting director can design the lighting plot for the studio set. The set design gives the bird's eye view of the set to which the director has added the camera placement, and the titling/opening design gives the requirements from the producer's point of view of some expected visualization. *Visualization* is the process of composing the content of a camera shot. The lighting director adds the lighting concept. (See the lighting plot form.)

FIGURE 2–8
The lighting plot. The lighting director creates the lighting plot from the director's blocking plot. Light instruments are chosen and placed and directed.

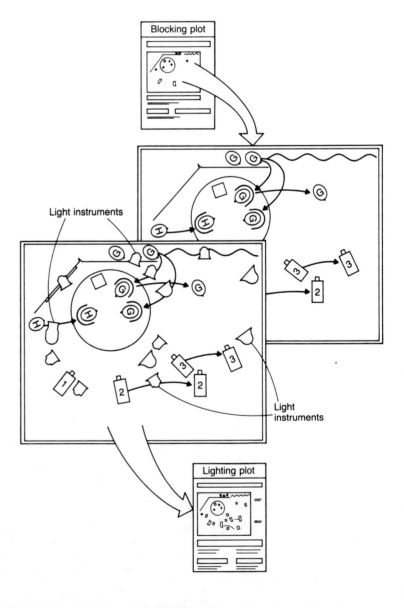

Submitting the lighting plot design to the producer and director for approval (LD 4)   The lighting director must submit the lighting plot to both the producer and the director for approval. Approval from the producer authorizes any expenses required to complete the lighting design in the studio.

Making the studio camera shot lists and distributing them to the camera operators (D 5)   The director breaks down the camera blocking plot to create the shot lists for each camera. These shot lists provide by number the basic defined shots and camera placement for each camera. These lists limit the coverage of the set and talent to the positions of the cameras and give the director a point of reference for each camera during videotape production of the program. Each camera has its own unduplicated camera shot and framing and its own limited area of the studio within which to function during production. (See the camera shot list form.)

Studying the program format and preproduction script (AD 2)   The assistant director spends preproduction time, especially before rehearsal(s) begin, studying the program format and preproduction script. These documents provide the assistant director with the requirements of studio production as well as begin to define the role that the assistant director can create to best aid the director during rehearsal(s) and videotaping.

Approving the audio and lighting plots and authorizing expenses and purchases (P 14)   The producer reviews the audio and lighting plots with an eye to any changes that might be made and then approves the designs. Approving the plots authorizes the audio director and the lighting director to begin constructing the designs and making the purchases necessary to complete the designs for program production.

Approving the audio and lighting plot designs (D 6)   The director reviews, makes changes to or recommendations for, and approves the audio and lighting designs for implementation. The sooner these designs are executed, the sooner rehearsal(s) can begin. Given completion dates, the director can schedule a production meeting to review the whole production process and inform production crew members of roles, rehearsal schedule, and production videotaping.

Overseeing studio set construction (D 7)   The director should oversee the construction of the studio set from the producer's design. Overseeing construction places the director at a point of control of the progress and of any changes in design that may affect the studio production of the program. Any changes from physical design to set color should be conveyed to the production crew to whom it may matter; e.g., color changes affect lighting design. The director should have a firm deadline for completion of set construction. Audio and lighting cannot implement their designs until the set is complete. Rehearsal(s) cannot be scheduled until the set is complete.

Familiarizing self with the program format and pre-production script (TD 2)   The technical director prepares for a production meeting and eventual rehearsal by studying the program format and the preproduction script. These documents should be comprehensive enough at this stage of preproduction to indicate some of the picturization demands of switching the program during rehearsal(s) and videotaping. At least these documents will alert the technical director to the questions to be asked during the production meeting before rehearsal.

Working with the program format and the shot lists (CO 2)   The camera operators prepare for both the production meeting and rehearsal(s) by studying the program format and the shot lists. These documents orient the camera operators to expected roles during rehearsal(s) and videotaping. Any questions generated by the format or shot lists should be asked during the production meeting.

Designing character generator and credits copy (P 15)   The producer is at a stage of preproduction that the character generator copy is ready to be created. The character generator copy includes the academy leader slate information as well as closing credits. (See the character generator copy form.)

Securing character generator text copy from the producer (PA 2)   Before a production meeting, the production assistant secures the character generator text copy from the producer. Any questions concerning the copy can be handled during the production meeting.

Reviewing and studying the program format form (TC 2)   The telecine operator studies the program format form received from the director to determine the film sources required for the program's production. The film source needs will indicate what film sources will have to be provided to the telecine operator by the producer or director.

Reviewing the program format for the order of production elements (TO 2)   The teleprompter operator reviews the program format for the order of the production elements prior to the production meeting and for a clearer definition of the studio prompter needs for the program.

Obtaining required copyright clearances, royalty rights, and synchronization rights (P 16)   The producer obtains any copyright clearances necessary for copyrighted material that may be planned for use in the program. Royalty rights and payments may also be due to performed materials (usually for plays or excerpts from plays). The music that guests may plan to use in an entertainment program may be copyrighted, and clearance to use it must be obtained. Most clearances have to be made in advance by mail or fax.

If copyrighted music, for instance, is to become part of the theme of the program, synchronization rights as well as copyright clearance are required. Synchronization rights are required because the copyrighted music is being wedded to another medium, in this case videotape. In television, visual images are being added to the prerecorded music. (This is unlike the case of radio, which simply plays copyrighted music.) A producer should

FIGURE 2–9
Producer's legal responsibilities. The producer has important legal obligations to perform for the program. Performance and synchronization rights, copyright clearances, and insurance coverage have to be secured.

Producer

expect to have to pay for the rights and often a considerable sum.

For most producers, the best route for music use is either to have original music written and recorded or to purchase original music from a music library publishing company. In many ways, this is the best and least expensive way to go.

Holding a production meeting with the studio production crew (D 8) The director holds a production meeting with the entire production crew before beginning program rehearsal(s). The production meeting is not the same as either the meetings held individually with each crew member or the initial crew meeting held with the whole crew. This meeting is held after production roles have been defined and crew personnel have had an opportunity to study preproduction documents relating to their role responsibilities. The production meeting is a forum for the director to tie all production elements together before attempting a rehearsal. This is the opportunity for the director to set program goals and objectives for the crew and to create a working relationship as a whole. Earlier individual meetings served to define specific role expectations. This production meeting is the time to announce a rehearsal schedule and to set goals for the rehearsal(s). This is also a forum for trouble-shooting anticipated problems during production.

For the crew, the production meeting is a forum to ask specific production related questions.

Attending the production meeting (T 4) The talent attends the production meeting as the first opportunity to meet the entire production crew. This is the opportunity for the talent to ask any production questions relating to the program, rehearsal(s), and studio videotaping.

Attending the production meeting (AD 3) The assistant director attends the production meeting, which helps the assistant director to define the assistant director's role for the production crew and talent and the relationship to the director.

Assisting the director (AD 4) Once the role and relationship of the assistant director to the director is clear to the crew, the assistant director gets more actively involved in assisting the director. Much depends on how the director wishes to structure the role of the assistant director and the extent of assistance needed during rehearsal(s) and program videotaping.

Attending the production meeting (F 3) The floor director attends the production meeting. The meeting defines the floor director's role and expectations from the production, the crew, and the talent, and the relationship to the director during production.

Attending the production meeting (TD 3) The technical director attends the production meeting. The technical director takes this opportunity to ask production questions relating to the picturization of the program and the technical director's role as program switcher.

Attending the production meeting (CO 3) The camera operators attend the production meeting. This is the opportunity for the camera operators to clarify their camera shots and framing from the shot lists and to ask questions about their role for the program's production.

Studying camera placement (CO 4) The camera operators study the placement of their cameras in the studio set as their remaining task in preproduction before rehearsal(s).

Attending the production meeting (A 6) The audio director attends the production meeting. The audio director elaborates for the director and the crew the expectations the audio director has for sound pickup and microphone use, and prerecorded voice-over tracks for the production of the program. Any questions relating to the audio coverage and recording of the program should be addressed to the audio director.

Attending the production meeting (LD 5) The lighting director attends the production meeting. This gives the lighting director the chance to present the lighting design to the crew and to ask and be asked questions about the program's lighting design and effects.

Lighting the completed studio set (LD 6) The lighting director now creates the approved lighting design on the completed studio set.

Attending the production meeting (PA 3) The production assistant attends the production meeting and can take this chance to clear up any problems or clarify the content of the screen text for the program.

Entering character generator copy for the program (PA 4) The production assistant begins to enter the character generator information copy into the character generator in preparation for the first rehearsal.

Attending the production meeting (TO 3) The teleprompter operator attends the production meeting to clarify the prompter's role in the program's production.

Setting up the teleprompter bed (TO 4) The teleprompter operator prepares for the first rehearsal by setting the prompter hardware bed in order for studio operation.

Attending the production meeting (TC 3) The telecine operator attends the production meeting. This gives the telecine operator the opportunity to better define and clarify the role the telecine plays in the program production.

Securing the film sources from the producer and/or the graphic artist (TC 4) The telecine operator secures any film sources required for the first rehearsal and later videotapings. The producer (or graphic artist who may have been hired to create special graphics) will have the film sources for the telecine.

Determining video playback requirements needed during the production and the order of any videotape playback (VTRO 2) The videotape recorder operator determines video playback requirements from the program format. This will have to be reviewed during the production meeting and in preparation for securing the playback videotapes for the rehearsal(s) and videotaping.

Checking the operation of video recorders and playback units (VTRO 3) The videotape recorder operator is responsible for checking the operation of any record or playback videotape decks scheduled for the rehearsal(s) and production videotaping for proper record and playback operation and video quality.

Performing preventive maintenance on videotape decks (VTRO 4) The videotape recorder operator performs regular preproduction maintenance on any videotape decks to be used for the rehearsal(s) and production. The simple procedure of cleaning recording and playback heads should be done before each rehearsal and videotaping.

Attending the production meeting (VTRO 5) The videotape recorder operator attends the production meet-

ing for the opportunity to clarify the videotape recording and playback requirements of the program during rehearsal(s) and production videotaping.

Securing the master videotapes for A-roll and B-roll from the producer (VTRO 6) The videotape recorder operator secures the B-roll playback videotapes for playback into the program during rehearsal(s) and production videotaping from the producer. The playback set-up required for A-rolling and B-rolling into the program can be determined from the program format form.

Choosing videotape playback and videotape record decks (VTRO 7) The videotape recorder operator sets the number and order of playback and record videotape deck requirements. The technical director will have to be informed of the videotape deck assignments for routing through the control room switcher and monitors.

Determining the videotape stock needs for production (VTRO 8) The videotape recorder operator determines the videotape stock that may be required for the production of the program during rehearsal(s) as well as during the whole telecast season of program units.

Checking the studio cameras with the camera operators (VEG 1) The video engineer has the preproduction responsibility of turning the studio cameras on and checking the cameras with the camera operators before rehearsal(s) and production videotaping.

Doing preventive maintenance on the cameras (VEG 2) During studio camera check the video engineer performs preventive maintenance on the cameras. Preventive maintenance can range from increasing the air pressure for the camera pedestal to back focusing the lens.

Securing the teleprompter script copy from the producer for use during rehearsal(s) (TO 5) The teleprompter operator secures the studio prompter script for the program from the producer.

Preparing to run some script copy for a camera monitor test (TO 6) The teleprompter operator prepares to run some script copy to test the camera prompter monitors. The video engineer will assist the prompter operator with this test.

Checking the teleprompter monitors on the studio cameras (VEG 3) The video engineer takes time during preproduction, with the help of the prompter operator, to check the proper functioning and adjustments of the prompter monitors on the front of the studio cameras.

Uncapping the camera lenses (VEG 4) The video engineer decides when the cameras are safely locked down or in the hands of the camera operators so the lenses of the cameras can be uncapped.

Setting video levels and lens apertures with studio lights (VEG 5) With lenses uncapped, the cameras locked down and focused on the same test area, and studio lights at production intensity levels, the video engineer sets the video levels and chooses a basic lens

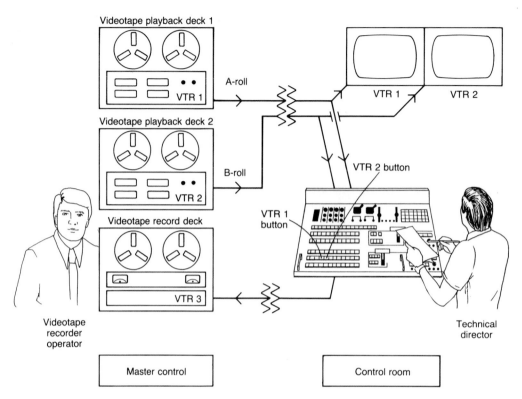

FIGURE 2–10
A-roll and B-roll videotape for the program. Inserting another video source into the program requires A-roll and B-roll preparation. This involves the videotape recorder operator and the technical director.

aperture setting for each camera. These are the settings that the video engineer will monitor throughout the rehearsal(s) and videotaping.

Routing the external video signal to camera monitors for camera operator use during rehearsal(s) and production (VEG 6)   The video engineer routes the external video signal from the control room to the cameras. This external signal allows the camera operators to choose to monitor the control room program line in order to facilitate talent framing during studio production and videotaping.

Checking the tally light operation on the cameras (VEG 7)   The video engineer checks the tally light operation before rehearsal(s) begin. A program requires accurate tally light operation because talent will frequently address the audience by looking directly into the camera lens. Tally light operation will permit the talent to know which camera is on line and when.

Reviewing the studio set lighting plot with the director (LD 7)   When the lighting director has completed the lighting plot design for the studio set, the lighting

FIGURE 2–11
Script copy prompting. Prompter script copy is prepared in one long strip. The script copy is fed over the prompter bed under the light and the camera lens. The monitor attached to the front of the studio camera projects the script copy in a reflected image to the talent.

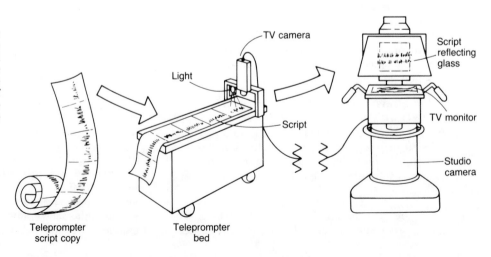

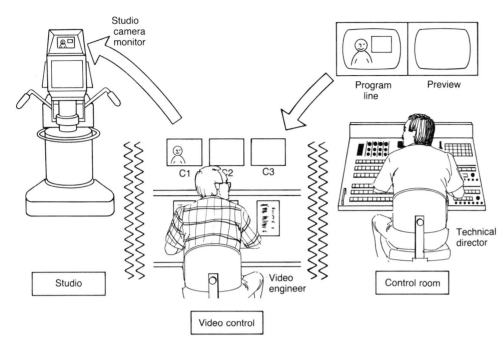

FIGURE 2-12
Routing the external signal to cameras. The video engineer routes the program line video signal to the studio cameras as an aid to the camera operators.

director reviews the plot with the director. Although the final test of the studio set lighting will be the rehearsal(s), the director has this prerehearsal opportunity to check the completed lighting design.

Reviewing the completed studio set lighting design with the lighting director (D 9) The director reviews the completed studio set lighting design with the lighting director. This is the opportunity for the director to walk the set and check the lighted areas for talent placement and talent movement during the program. Ultimately, the real test for the lighting design is going to be the rehearsal(s).

Trying make-up on and testing make-up under the studio set lights and on-camera (T 5) The talent tries on the make-up that will be required for the program. Testing make-up under set lights and on-camera before rehearsal firms up one element of the production that need not wait until rehearsal. It helps the crew's morale when the talent takes the lead in setting finished standards before the pressure and stress of rehearsal(s) and production. Make-up is one such element that could be settled before rehearsal.

Deciding wardrobe with the producer (T 6) Another production element that can be decided before rehearsal is the wardrobe choice for the talent. This is something that the talent and the producer decide. Style and color of clothes are strong production values, and the choices should not be left to whatever clothes are available. Checking the reproduction of style and color on-camera prior to rehearsal is a good idea.

Holding program rehearsal(s) and giving production critiques of the rehearsal(s) (D 10) The director schedules and holds rehearsal(s) for the program. Rehearsal(s) are important for everybody.

If the new program is to be aired live, many rehearsal(s) may be required. A norm for the number of rehearsals necessary for producing live programs should be one rehearsal per work day followed by extensive critiques from the director and the producer for about two weeks. Producers and directors might hire local professional actors and actresses to play the roles of guests during rehearsals as part of talent and crew training.

If the new program is to be videotaped with a later broadcast date, only a few rehearsals or a single rehearsal may be required. In the case of a tape-delayed program, the time after a studio videotaping session can be used for postproduction—to repair or change elements of the production before airing.

Producing or overseeing the availability of film sources, videotape sources, studio prompter script; and making talent wardrobe and make-up decisions for rehearsal(s) (P 17) The producer secures or oversees the production of those sources that will be needed for the program before rehearsal(s) begin. The sources include any film sources (35mm or 16mm), B-rolled videotape for playback into the program, and writing and typing the studio prompter script copy.

The producer also makes wardrobe and make-up decisions with the help of the talent for the program before rehearsal(s) begin.

Supervising and critiquing the program rehearsal(s) (P 18) The producer takes a supervisory role during rehearsal(s). A rehearsal works out production problems and trains the production crew to work together.

If the program is to air live, many rehearsal(s) may be needed. It would not be uncommon to rehearse a new program to be aired live for two weeks (i.e., ten program rehearsals).

For a program designed to be videotaped for later broadcast, one rehearsal may be sufficient. A videotaped program can be cleaned up in postproduction before

FIGURE 2–13
The director controls production. The director controls the process of program development with a flow of meetings, rehearsal(s), critique session(s), and crew calls.

Production meeting

Rehearsal

Critique session

Crew call

Production session

Director

Producer   Director

broadcast. Whether live or taped, any quality program can be improved by rehearsing in advance.

After a rehearsal is complete, both talent and production crew meet with the producer and the director for a critique session, with an aim toward improving the production.

Attending rehearsal(s) and critique session(s) (T 7) Talent is crucial to program rehearsal(s) and critique session(s), and talent should expect to perform for them. Talent should treat rehearsal(s) as a live program and give the best possible performance to assist the studio production crew. After rehearsal(s), talent should expect to be open to constructive criticism from both the producer and the director. It is from constructive criticism that any professional can hope to grow at his or her craft.

Working the program's rehearsal(s) and attending critique session(s) (AD 5) The assistant director works the defined role for the assistant director during rehearsal(s). A rehearsal is followed by a critique session where the videotape of the rehearsal is watched with the producer and director. The assistant director should pay attention to criticism that affects the role played by the assistant director during program production.

Working the program's rehearsal(s) and attending critique session(s) (F 4) The floor director works the role defined for the floor director during the program's rehearsal(s). After rehearsal(s), the production crew watches the videotape of the program and listens to the criticism from the producer and the director. The floor director should note the criticisms and problems originating from

the studio during rehearsal(s) and correct them during the following rehearsal(s) or during the program videotaping.

Working the program's rehearsal(s) and attending critique session(s) (TD 4) The technical director works the role defined for the technical director during the program's rehearsal(s). During the critique session following each rehearsal, the technical director should listen for those things the producer and director criticize that are directed to elements of the program for which the technical director is responsible. Changes are made during the next rehearsal or during the videotaping.

Working the program's rehearsal(s) and attending critique session(s) (CO 5) The camera operators work the rehearsal(s) as they would a videotaped production for broadcast. After each rehearsal, the camera operators, along with the other crew members, view the videotape of the rehearsal and listen as the producer and director offer criticism of the production in order to improve the program's production before telecast videotaping. This is the time for camera operators to contribute any insights, problems, and solutions to the director as ways to better the look of the program by improving the angle of the camera shots. Camera shots create the look of the program for the audience and are important to the success of the program.

Working the program's rehearsal(s) and attending critique session(s) (A 7) The audio director works the rehearsal(s) to test the audio design of the program. The rehearsal(s) become for the audio director the opportunity to see if the preproduction design functions or if the sound pickup design should be changed. The audio director should view the videotaped rehearsal(s) with the producer and the director and note their criticisms as part of improving the overall program production.

Working the program's rehearsal(s) and attending critique session(s) (LD 8)   The lighting director works the program's rehearsal(s) as the opportunity to check the lighting design of the set. The lighting director notes both the look of the rehearsal videotape and the criticisms from the producer and director. Lighting changes and adjustments are made before the next rehearsal or production videotaping.

Working the program's rehearsal(s) and attending critique session(s) (PA 5)   The production assistant works the program's rehearsal(s) and gauges the design and sequencing of character generator copy for the program. The opportunity to test the look of screen text copy before final production is advantageous. Text design and sequencing of screen texts can appear different when seen in the context of the whole program than when simply designed on paper or entered into the character generator. The production assistant should pay attention to those criticisms from the producer and director that pertain to the production and presentation of the character generator screen text copy.

Working the program's rehearsal(s) and attending critique session(s) (TO 7)   The teleprompter operator works the program rehearsal(s) if talent are required to read studio prompter copy. As with other production crew members, the prompter operator needs to know his or her role during rehearsal(s) and production videotaping and must listen to the criticisms from the producer and director and the talent during the rehearsal critique session(s). Improvements should be introduced during subsequent rehearsal(s) or production videotaping.

Working the program's rehearsal(s) and attending critique session(s) (TC 5)   The telecine operator works the program's rehearsal(s) and attends the postrehearsal critique session(s) with the producer and the director. Problems with the telecine and any film sources for the program should be raised and solutions found.

Working the program's rehearsal(s) and attending critique session(s) (VTRO 9)   The videotape recorder operator works the rehearsal(s) by B-rolling any prerecorded video sources into the program and recording the rehearsal(s). The videotaped rehearsal(s) are played back for the producer and the director. During the critique session(s) the videotape recorder operator should be sensitive to problems in the videotape area and search out solutions before the next rehearsal or production videotaping.

Working the program's rehearsal(s) and attending critique session(s) (VEG 8)   The video engineer works the rehearsal(s) and shares problems encountered with the cameras and their operation during the postrehearsal critique session(s) with the producer and the director. A person with the technical expertise of the video engineer is a good resource for the improvement of the video portion of the program.

Designing program promotions (P 19)   A remaining preproduction responsibility for the producer is to plan and design promotions for the new program. These promotions may include videotaped clips from good rehearsals or still photo sessions on the set with the talent. It may also mean inviting a local newspaper media reviewer to a rehearsal.

Setting crew call requirements (D 11)   With the last rehearsal, the director sets crew call time and place requirements for the production crew and talent. Assuming that the new program is expected to continue production indefinitely, a standard of prompt crew call attendance begins now.

THE PRODUCTION PROCESS

The studio production of the talk show/entertainment program is a genre of television studio production distinct from most other studio production genres.

Unlike television news, drama, and commercial production, the talk show/entertainment program genre has little or no scripted dialogue. The greater portion of the talk show/entertainment television program genre is ad-lib. *Ad-lib* is defined as speaking or performing without a script. This element of spontaneity survives only if the relationship between the talent and the control room director is good. The more the host, hostess, or moderator and the director work with and know each other, the better will be the studio videotaping session.

Another distinguishing characteristic of the talk show/entertainment program genre is first-time guests on the program who may not be familiar or comfortable with television studio production. These characteristics make the production of this genre more challenging and the number of preproduction rehearsals understandable.

The number of studio production crew personnel for the talk show/entertainment program is the smallest or at least the minimum required for studio operation. A producer, director, assistant director, technical director, audio director, production assistant, lighting director, and video engineer occupy the control room during talk show/entertainment program production; the talent, floor director, camera operators, and prompter operator occupy the studio; and the videotape recorder operator and telecine operator occupy the master control area of the production facility. The crew may not need a prompter operator or a telecine operator. In some operations, a director may also switch the program (replacing the technical director) and function without an assistant director. The lighting director, videotape recorder operator, and video engineer may be part of the production facility and not considered a part of the program production crew. That leaves a total program production crew of eight or nine (including the talent), the smallest number of personnel to be able to operate a production studio.

FIGURE 2–14
Crew placement assignment. This diagram places all production personnel in their respective positions during program production. The three areas of a production facility are the studio, the control room, and the master control area.

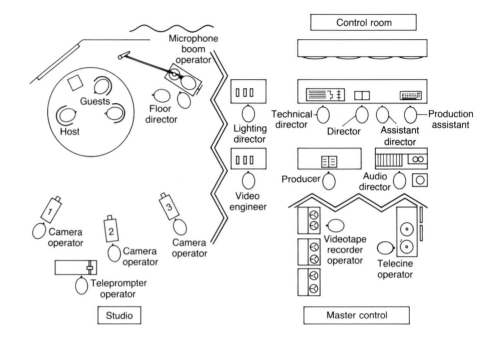

• **Personnel**

Producer (P) The producer is the program supervisor present during studio production for the program. Because the producer is responsible for the program, the producer is present in the control room to trouble-shoot any production problems and to clarify and answer any questions regarding elements of the program's format.

Talent (T) The talent is the center of the activity in the talk show/entertainment program production. The talent includes the host, hostess, or moderator, depending on the assigned role, and guests.

Director (D) The director is like the center of a wheel from whom all spokes radiate. Many see the director in television production as a conductor of an orchestra. Both analogies apply. The director is the center of and in the control of all of the individuals and activity that goes into producing a talk show/entertainment program. From the control room of the facility, with headset intercom connections to principal players, the director calls every change in video and audio signals.

Assistant director (AD) The assistant director plays a strong supporting role to the director during production. The assistant director has to know the format/rundown sheet; know all prerecorded times of B-roll video sets; and activate and read the times of all stop watches, timers, and counters measuring the front time to the program, the back times, and all segment times. The assistant director also keeps track of character generator copy readied for matte into the program.

Technical director (TD) The technical director is the principal technician who assembles the visual imaging of the production. The technical director responds to all the calls of the director and effects each video change throughout the program. Because this is an unscripted production

with a format/rundown sheet, the technical director should not anticipate a director's calls without the director's permission. This mutual working relationship develops over the course of preparing many programs.

Production assistant (PA) The production assistant is responsible to recall from the memory of the character generator any and all screen text copy entered from the character generator information copy list during preproduction.

Audio director (A) The audio director has the production responsibility to channel the live in-studio or prerecorded audio sources designed by the producer into the program production.

Floor director (F) The floor director functions during studio production as a stage director for talent and guests and the director's alter ego or second self. The floor director is the persona of the director in the studio, communicating and effecting the director's calls involving studio personnel, especially the talent. The floor director is responsible for communicating to the director the situation of the studio and its personnel during production.

Camera operators (CO) The camera operators perform the important role of providing the necessary studio originated video for the program. This means covering the talent during the talent's presentation of the program format/rundown sheet.

Teleprompter operator (TO) The script prompter operator has the responsibility to video and transmit to the talent the reading copy of the script or format/rundown order via camera mounted monitors during the program.

Telecine operator (TC) The telecine operator functions from the master control room where the telecine is usually located. The telecine holds those 35mm and 16mm film sources that will be used in the program. The telecine operator either operates the telecine manually or routes control remotely to the control room and to the assistant director.

Lighting director (LD) The lighting director is part of the studio production crew for purposes of monitoring the light levels on the set and talent and for changing the intensity of set lights should some dimming of the lights be part of the production values of the program.

Videotape recorder operator (VTRO) The videotape recorder operator is in the master control area of the television facility. The primary role of the videotape recorder operator is to cue up and roll all playback videotape sources for B-rolling into the program and the record deck should the program be recorded as well as telecast.

Video engineer (VEG) The video engineer monitors all studio cameras during production. The video engineer has to adjust the lens aperture setting as light levels change during production. The video engineer also monitors soft focus from the cameras.

• Production Stages

Supervising talent and crew calls and meeting with the director, talent, and crew (P 1) The producer begins the studio preparation production process by supervising the talent and crew calls scheduled by the director at this production meeting. The crew call (and talent call) is a scheduled gathering or rendezvous time for all production personnel. Supervisory personnel might use the crew call as a time for an updated production meeting. The talent and crew calls may be a joint or a separate meeting time. Talent may need more or less lead time to be ready for studio production (e.g., make-up or wardrobe). This may entail an earlier or later talent call.

The studio production crew needs enough lead time to be thoroughly prepared when talent are ready. Studio production is often characterized as a "hurry up and wait" phenomenon. Adequate crew call lead time can remedy that for the talent of a program.

Crew call is an opportunity for the producer and director to convey last minute details and/or changes in production that pertain to the crew and talent. Guest changes or content changes can be made as late as crew call time for a production session.

Distributing the format/rundown sheet of the program unit being produced (P 2) A primary requirement for the program being produced is the format/rundown sheet for the program. The format/rundown sheet is a listing of the contents of the order of elements that make up the program being produced. The format/rundown sheet is the filled out program specific format form. It contains names of guests, content of each guest unit, length of each guest unit, and special production requirements (e.g., film, slides, or video). Most production crew members and the talent need copies of the format/rundown sheet. The producer is responsible for develop-

ing the format/rundown sheet and for distributing copies of the sheet to the director, crew, and talent at crew call.

Holding scheduled talent and crew calls and receiving the format/rundown sheet (D 1) The director begins the studio production session by meeting with both talent and crew at either joint or separate calls. The director receives the format/rundown sheet from the producer and distributes copies of the sheet to the production crew and talent.

The director uses this crew call as the opportunity to set expectations for the program's production. This includes announcing changes to the program format or any other special production element, announcing crew or facility changes, and answering any questions the crew or talent may have concerning the production and their roles.

If the program is being videotaped for later telecast, the director concludes crew call by setting a time convenient to the crew for set-up and the talent for wardrobe and make-up preparation. If the program is broadcast live, real clock air time determines studio and equipment set-up and talent preparation time.

Reviewing the format/rundown sheet for program elements and update (D 2) The director reviews the format/rundown sheet with the production crew for additions to the program's elements and any other update for the current program production session.

Meeting with the producer and director for crew call or talent call (T 1) The host, hostess, or moderator of the program meets during the scheduled crew call or talent call with the producer and the director. The talent receives the format/rundown sheet for the particular program unit being produced.

Meeting with the producer and the director for crew call and receiving a copy of the format/rundown sheet for the program unit (AD 1) The assistant director meets with the producer and the director for crew call. The assistant director receives a copy of the format/rundown sheet for the program unit and takes notes for the director during the rest of the meeting.

Meeting with the producer and the director for crew call (A 1) The audio director meets with the producer and the director for crew call. The audio director receives a copy of the format/rundown sheet for the scheduled program unit being produced during the current production session.

Meeting with the producer and the director for crew call (F 1) The floor director meets with the producer and the director for crew call. The floor director receives a copy of the format/rundown sheet for the program unit being produced.

Meeting with the producer and the director for crew call (CO 1) The camera operators meet for crew call with the producer and the director. They each receive a copy of the format/rundown sheet for the scheduled program unit being produced.

Meeting with the producer and the director for crew call (TD 1)   The technical director meets with both the producer and the director for crew call. The technical director receives a copy of the format/rundown sheet for the scheduled program unit being produced.

Meeting with the producer and the director for crew call (LD 1)   The lighting director meets with the producer and the director for crew call. The lighting director receives a copy of the format/rundown sheet for the program unit being produced.

Meeting with the producer and the director for crew call (PA 1)   The production assistant meets with the producer and the director for crew call. The production assistant receives a copy of the format/rundown sheet for the program being produced.

Meeting with the producer and the director for crew call (TO 1)   The teleprompter operator meets with the producer and the director for crew call. The prompter operator receives a copy of the format/rundown sheet for the program unit being produced during the current production session.

Meeting with the producer and the director for crew call (TC 1)   The telecine operator meets for crew call with the producer and the director. The telecine operator receives a copy of the format/rundown sheet for the scheduled program unit being produced.

Meeting with the producer and the director for crew call (VTRO 1)   The videotape recorder operator meets with the producer and the director for crew call. The videotape recorder operator receives a copy of the format/rundown sheet for the program unit being produced during the current production session.

Meeting with the producer and the director for crew call (VEG 1)   The video engineer meets with the producer and the director for crew call. The video engineer receives a copy of the format/rundown sheet for the program unit being produced during the current production session.

Reviewing the format/rundown sheet for studio microphone needs, prerecorded audio sources, and playback audio needs and updates (A 2)   The audio director keeps abreast of any additions or updates to the program format/rundown sheet for additional microphones in the studio, additional prerecorded audio sources, or additional playback audio feeds through the audio board for the production.

Checking the format/rundown sheet for last minute updates, monitoring crew readiness, and preparing and assisting the director with preprogram details (AD 2)   The assistant director remains at the side of the director and assists in any task that facilitates the beginning of production. The best assistance is knowledge of the format/rundown sheet.

The assistant director keeps abreast of all format/rundown sheet updates and informs the director. The assistant director keeps tabs on the state of readiness of the production crew.

Reviewing the format/rundown sheet for order of program updates (F 2)   The floor director reviews the format/rundown sheet for updates or changes in the order of the program that affect the studio set and studio personnel, crew, talent, and guests.

Reviewing the format/rundown sheet for order of program updates (PA 2)   The production assistant reviews the format/rundown sheet for updates or changes in the order of the program that affect the character generator content or order of information.

Reviewing the format/rundown sheet for order of program updates (TC 2)   The telecine operator reviews the format/rundown sheet for updates or changes in the order of the program that affect the film sources in the telecine.

Reviewing the format/rundown sheet for order of program updates (TD 2)   The technical director reviews the format/rundown sheet for updates or changes in the order of the program that affect the picturization of the program and the technical director's requirements at the production switcher.

Reviewing the format/rundown sheet for studio camera needs, changes, updates (CO 2)   The camera operators apprise themselves of changes and updates to their studio performance requirements.

Distributing film sources, prompter script, updated character generator copy, and B-roll videotape (P 3)   The producer takes the opportunity of having the production crew together to distribute resources necessary for the program's production. The telecine operator requires any film sources for the program (35mm or 16mm film), the prompter operator and talent need the script copy, the production assistant needs any character generator information copy updates, and the videotape recorder operator needs any videotape that will be B-rolled into the program during production. All of these resources are the responsibility of the producer.

Supervising final studio facility and set arrangements (D 3)   The director walks through the studio production facility and the studio set as a final detail check before and while the crew sets up for production videotaping. This gives the director the opportunity to alert the producer to anything missing or not yet in place for production. The director oversees all equipment set-up for the production. The sooner the director reviews crew positions and checks the hardware and operation conditions, the sooner the director can retire to the control room to begin production checks. The breadth of personnel and equipment that has to converge into the moment of beginning videotaping is extensive. The director must be aware of missing or malfunctioning hardware or other difficulties, so the producer can trouble-shoot and solve the problems.

The crew should be encouraged to bring any difficulties

in production elements to the attention of the director and the producer as soon as possible.

Handling studio facility and studio set arrangements (P 4)   The producer follows through with the role responsibility for the producer from preproduction and checks for expected arrangements determined and ordered during preproduction from the production facility. This includes everything from air conditioning in the studio to the set's dressing. The producer initiates facility relations before production and maintains the relationship with facility supervisory personnel during production. Any additional requests and changes regarding the production facility should go through the producer.

Supervising equipment set-up and placement (D 4)   Besides supervising the studio and studio set arrangement, the director also supervises equipment set-up and where equipment is placed. Cameras, teleprompter bed, and telecine are equipment hardware that require a director's early supervision to avoid problem delays later in program videotaping preparation.

Reviewing the format/rundown sheet for program order, changes, or updates (T 2)   The talent checks the format/rundown sheet for any updates or changes that involve the talent's performance.

Securing talent copy of the script (T 3)   The talent for the program must secure a copy of the studio prompter script from the producer. This is necessary only if the program requires script copy to be read by the talent during program videotaping.

Meeting with the guest(s) scheduled for the program unit being produced (P 5)   The producer meets with the guest(s) scheduled for the program when they arrive at the production facility. The guests need the time with the producer to establish their roles before production and during program videotaping. The producer walks the guest(s) through the format/rundown sheet. The producer will also have to see to make-up requirements for the guest(s), which may be as simple as a powdering with translucent powder. The talent might also be able to apply pancake make-up base and powder to the guest(s) if necessary.

Handling production crew, talent, and guest(s) details (P 6)   The producer handles personal details for the talent, guest(s), and crew. This can entail anything from parking for personal cars and storage for securities during production to providing hot water in the make-up room and coffee in the green room.

Assuming responsibility for the studio, set, talent, guest(s), and studio production crew during studio use (F 3)   After the director has made a check of the studio and equipment, the floor director takes responsibility for everything and everyone who functions in the studio. This includes the studio itself, the program's set, the talent and guest(s), and the production crew (mainly, the camera operators). The floor director encourages the crew to get ready and prepares to get the talent and guest(s) to the set when the director is ready.

If there is a studio audience, the floor director is responsible for them, which may include prepping the audience to the excitement of the program.

Beginning studio audio equipment set-up (A 3)   The audio director begins studio audio set-up immediately after crew call and a review of the format/rundown sheet.

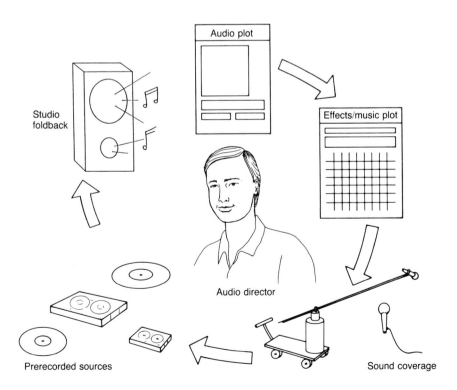

Audio plot

Studio foldback

Effects/music plot

Audio director

Prerecorded sources

Sound coverage

FIGURE 2–15
The audio director. During production, the audio director is responsible for creating the audio plot and for accounting for all sound effects and music, all prerecorded audio sources, sound coverage from the studio, and the need for foldback in the studio during production.

FIGURE 2–16
Audio patching. The audio director patches microphones into input receptors in the studio, patches those input sources into the audio control board, and prepares to set gain and tone levels.

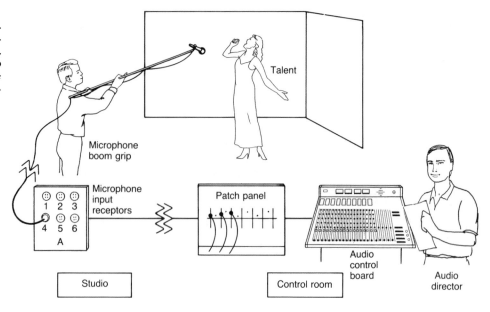

The audio director places microphones on the set for the talent (host, hostess, or moderator) and each scheduled guest(s). For a talk show format, some form of lavaliere may be used or a platform boom directional microphone will be used. For an entertainment program format, handheld microphones may be planned and/or the platform boom directional microphone used. These microphones have to be set in place.

Running microphone cables and recording studio microphone inputs (A 4)   The audio director runs microphone cables from the microphones required for the program. These cable runs have to avoid high traffic areas and especially any guest performing area of the studio. Once cables are run, the microphone input receptors have to be recorded for patching in the control room at the audio console.

Patching microphone cable inputs into the audio control board in the control room (A 5)   The audio director patches the corresponding audio cable studio inputs into the audio control board in the control room. This patching permits the audio director to operate and control the audio signal from the respective studio microphones.

Reading the script for familiarity and pronunciation problems (T 4)   The talent reads the script checking that the typed copy reads with a style and grammatical familiarity and that there are no word pronunciation problems. If there are, correction and proper pronunciation should be checked with the producer.

Marking the teleprompter copy of the script for reading interpretation (T 5)   The talent marks the teleprompter script copy for reading interpretation and the correct pronunciation of difficult words. Talent should be aware that generally we are more visually literate (i.e., we recognize with the eye more vocabulary words) than we really know how to pronounce (i.e., we may never have vocalized some words). This breeds a tendency to

think that we can read some words properly. Talent should never guess at the pronunciation of words. Break down into syllables, phoneticize, and accentuate all unfamiliar words on the space above the typed words on the prompter script copy.

Reviewing the format/rundown sheet for the program order and any changes in lighting needs (LD 2)   The lighting director needs to be alerted to any changes in the order of the program and those changes that affect studio set lighting requirements.

Checking the lighting pattern on the studio set and lighting instruments (LD 3)   The lighting director checks the studio set for the lighting pattern designed on the lighting plot for the set. Part of checking the set lighting includes checking each designated light instrument.

Reviewing the format/rundown sheet for changes and/or updates that affect camera engineering (VEG 2)   The video engineer reviews the format/rundown sheet for the program being produced for any indication of changes and/or updates that affect the performance of the cameras or camera engineering needs.

Readying the studio cameras for lens shading and videotaping (VEG 3)   The video engineer, working with the camera operators, readies the studio cameras for lens shading in preparation for videotaping. This requires setting the cameras in place in the studio before the set, turning the set lighting on, and aiming and framing all three cameras on a test chart placed in the lighted set by the video engineer.

Setting up and preparing assigned cameras for placement and engineer shading (CO 3)   The camera operators work with the video engineer and prepare their cameras for the electronic shading of the camera lens. The camera operators place their cameras in front of the lighted set in the studio and aim and focus on a test chart placed in the lighted area of the set by the video engineer.

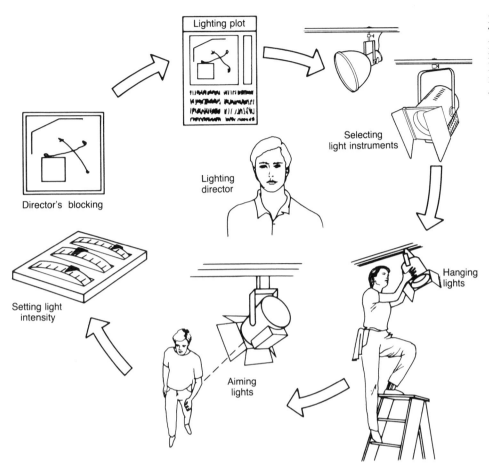

FIGURE 2–17
The lighting director. During production, the lighting director is responsible for creating the lighting plot and checking all light instruments, light instrument aiming, and light intensity.

Labels in figure: Lighting plot; Director's blocking; Lighting director; Selecting light instruments; Setting light intensity; Aiming lights; Hanging lights

Checking video levels of cameras with the lighting on the set (VEG 4) The video engineer checks the video levels of the camera lenses of all three studio cameras by setting the lends aperture of each.

Alerting the director when ready (VEG 5) The video engineer alerts the director when the cameras are ready for videotape production.

Reviewing the camera shot list and attaching the list to the camera (CO 4) The camera operators review their camera shot lists for the camera shots and framing for which they are responsible. The shot lists are then attached to the clipboard area behind the cameras under the camera monitor.

Checking lighting effects over control room monitors (LD 4) As part of checking overall set lighting, the lighting director needs to see, over control room monitors, how the whole set looks with the studio set lights on.

Checking for unwanted light reflection on the teleprompter monitors (LD 5) The lighting director checks the teleprompter monitors on each camera for unwanted light reflections and glare from studio lights before production.

Making lighting intensity or light instrument changes (LD 6) The lighting director makes those changes that correct unwanted light glare studio reflections by altering light intensity or re-aiming instruments.

Alerting the director when lighting is ready (LD 7) The lighting director informs the director when the studio set lighting is ready for videotape production.

Securing updated character generator copy from the producer (PA 3) The production assistant secures updated character generator text copy from the producer at crew call.

Entering and recording last minute data and other changes into the character generator (PA 4) The production assistant may receive last minute additions or changes to the character generator copy. Existing data will have to be changed or updated.

Checking intercom network connections (PA 5) The production assistant checks the intercom network connections needed during production. The production assistant needs intercom connection with the assistant director. Being in communication with the director and technical director could also be of some advantage to a production assistant.

Reviewing the format/rundown sheet for changes and/or updates that affect the teleprompter operator (TO 2) The teleprompter operator reviews the format/rundown sheet to discover any changes or updates to the format/rundown of the program that affect the order of program elements or the script for the talent.

Securing the teleprompter script copy from the producer (TO 3)   The script prompter operator secures the prompter copy of the production script from the producer after crew call.

Preparing teleprompter script copy for the teleprompter bed (TO 4)   The prompter operator takes the copy of the script and places it on the teleprompter bed. Under the teleprompter video camera, the script is reproduced over the monitors on the front of the studio cameras.

Checking the video reproduction of the script from the teleprompter bed to the camera monitors (TO 5)   The teleprompter operator checks that the teleprompter script reproduces acceptably on the monitors on the front of the studio cameras. In some cases, the camera monitor requires adjustment for contrast and brightness.

Permitting talent to check reading pleasure, practice with the script, and check the foldback sound in the studio (TO 6)   The teleprompter operator takes this opportunity to permit the talent to check both the reading height of text on the teleprompter screen and speed of the script. During this practice, the prompter operator checks the volume level of studio foldback so the talent voice can be heard adequately for the prompter operator to follow with the script.

Meeting the program guest(s) and audience (T 6)   The talent—host, hostess, or moderator—takes time before going to the studio to meet the guest(s) scheduled for the program. This gives the guest(s) an opportunity to meet the host, hostess, or moderator before they meet on the set. This is simply a chance to be introduced.

If a studio audience is part of the studio production, the talent may need to be introduced and meet the audience before production begins. The time the talent spends with a studio audience helps generate enthusiasm and excitement for both the program talent as well as the audience.

Alerting the floor director when ready (TO 7)   The teleprompter operator informs the floor director when the script and the prompter are ready.

Securing any film sources from the producer (TC 3)   The telecine operator secures any film sources from the producer after crew call. These film sources will have to be loaded into the telecine before production.

Loading the telecine with 35mm slides or 16mm film as necessary (TC 4)   The telecine operator loads the telecine with whatever film sources—35mm slides or 16mm film—are going to be used during the program production.

Checking the telecine for proper operation and correct order of film sources (TC 5)   The telecine operator makes a final check on the operation of the telecine—manual operation (if the telecine operator will advance film sources during production) or remote operation (if the assistant director will advance film sources during production)—choices. A final check should be made of the order of film sources, especially 35mm slides, in the telecine.

Checking intercom network connections (TC 6)   The telecine operator needs intercom connection with the

FIGURE 2–18
Talent preparation. The host or hostess for the program moves steadily through pretaping preparation from cast call, reviewing guest information, dressing, putting on make-up, meeting guests, practicing reading prompter copy, and following the program format/rundown.

director and the assistant director, and these connections should be checked.

Communicating readiness to the assistant director (TC 7) The telecine operator alerts the assistant director when the telecine and film sources are ready for production.

Reviewing the format/rundown sheet for any changes and/or updates that affect the videotape recorder operator (VTRO 2) The videotape recorder operator reviews the format/rundown sheet for any changes and/or updates that affect the B-roll videotape or any other element (e.g., order of elements) in the program.

Securing any B-roll videotape from the producer (VTRO 3) The videotape recorder operator secures any required B-roll videotape from the producer after crew call.

Choosing and preparing the record and playback videotape decks, selecting videotape recording stock, and threading record and playback videotape decks for B-rolling and recording (VTRO 4) The videotape recorder operator prepares for videotaping by choosing the record videotape deck for recording and the playback deck for B-rolling.

The videotape stock to be recorded is chosen and the record deck is threaded in preparation for recording the program.

Checking intercom connections (VTRO 5) The videotape recorder operator checks those intercom connections that will be needed by the videotape recorder operator during production. Principally, the videotape recorder operator needs intercom connection with the director, technical director, and assistant director.

Alerting the technical director of record and playback deck assignment for signal routing (VTRO 6) Once record and playback decks are prepared by the videotape recorder operator, the videotape recorder operator notifies the technical director of the record and playback deck assignments so correct signal routing through the switcher can be made.

Checking intercom network connections (TD 3) The technical director requires some intercom connections during the production, and each of these has to be checked for connection and crew response. The best check is to ask for a crew response. The technical director has contact with the videotape recorder operator, director, and assistant director during production.

Checking with the videotape recorder operator for video playback routing through the switcher (TD 4) The technical director checks with the videotape recorder operator for the routed video source through the switcher. The technical director then hits the assigned buttons on the switcher and has the assistant director (if the playback decks are operated remotely) or videotape recorder operator (if the playback decks are operated manually) roll each deck and visually check the response.

Setting up the switcher for required effects and testing the effects (TD 5) The technical director sets up the switcher for any effects that will be required during the program production. The effects are set up and tested visually over the control room monitors.

Checking the video levels of videotape playback sources with the videotape recorder operator (TD 6) While rolling all videotape playback sources to check routing, the technical director also checks the video levels of each B-roll video source. Video levels are checked through vectorscopes at the switcher. If levels do not read at acceptable levels, the videotape recorder operator makes adjustments in master control until video level readings are acceptable to the technical director.

Setting video levels of video playback sources with the technical director (VTRO 7) The videotape recorder operator responds to the technical director as each video source is checked by running some of the video until the technical director affirms acceptable video levels of each video through the switcher. The videotape recorder operator adjusts the video levels on each playback deck while the technical director reads the levels from the vectorscope at the switcher.

Switching the remote control of playback videotape decks to the control room and the assistant director (VTRO 8) The videotape recorder operator switches the remote control of playback videotape decks to the control room and the assistant director if this is required.

Alerting the director when ready (VTRO 9) The videotape recorder operator alerts the director when all elements of the master control are ready for videotape production.

Alerting the director when ready (TD 7) The technical director alerts the director when all checks and presets are ready and the technical director is ready to begin production videotaping.

Checking camera for the zoom, pan, tilt, dolly, truck, pedestal, and arc control (CO 5) The camera operators take the moments before production begins to make a fast run through the principal movements of their cameras. These movements include the zoom, pan, tilt, dolly, truck, pedestal, and arc.

Securing adequate camera cable behind cameras for movement flexibility (CO 6) Each camera operator secures enough camera cable directly behind each camera to ensure adequate flexibility in camera movement without cable drag on the camera.

Checking intercom network connections (CO 7) The camera operators check their intercom network connections in order to hear the director's calls during production. The best check is to get a response from the director. The camera operators need only a one way connection during production: from the director to them.

Practicing required shots of the talent (CO 8) Camera operators take production preparation time to practice the defined shots of the talent that will be required during production. Fast camera movements (camera breaks) should also be practiced.

Checking lens filter choice (CO 9) The camera operators make a final check that the correct filter has been chosen and is properly in place before the camera lens. This implies that a filter is required for some production value during the program (e.g., a star filter for shooting studio lights). In some instances, the visual effect will not be noticed clearly enough over the camera monitor and the camera operators will have to check with the video engineer who has a more accurate reading of a filter in place.

Maintaining depth of field focus during and after changes in camera position (CO 10) The camera operators need practice and reminders to correct depth of field changes whenever the camera changes position during production. Camera operators need the practice of camera movements and the rapid zoom-in to refocus and zoom-out to reestablish the defined shot. Fine focusing should also be practiced.

Setting opening shots and alerting the director of readiness (CO 11) The camera operators indicate their readiness to begin production by setting their respective opening shots on their cameras and altering the director.

Monitoring the program from the control room during production (P 7) The producer needs to be closer to the program's production given the valuable resource the producer is to the format/rundown of the production. The best place for the producer to monitor the production is from the control room in open communication with the director.

Retiring to the control room (D 5) After details of studio set-up are complete, the director retires to the control room to begin last minute checks before production videotaping.

Orienting to assigned video source monitors (D 6) The director needs to take a moment and orient to any new (as well as old) video source monitor assignments to the wall of monitors facing the control room staff.

Orienting to the video source monitors (AD 3) The assistant director also orients to all of the video source monitors facing the control room staff during production.

Checking the intercom network connections and response stations (D 7) The director checks (or assigns) all intercom network connections important to the director during studio production. The best way to check is to call each intercom station and exact a response.

Checking all intercom network connections (AD 4) The assistant director checks all of the intercom network connections that are important to the assistant director. The best check is to elicit a response from the crew members on the intercom.

Preparing and assisting the director with the format/ rundown sheet and production crew readiness (AD 5) The assistant director prepares to assist the director. This involves being aware of changes and/or updates on the format/rundown sheet for the program being produced. It also includes assisting the director in achieving the readiness of production crew personnel, which may involve trouble-shooting for the respective crew personnel having difficulty achieving a state of readiness for production. One crew member can hold up the entire production crew for unnecessary delays that could have been avoided by making the assistant director aware of problems earlier during preparation.

Reviewing recorded character generator information with the assistant director (PA 6) The production assistant should have the assistant director go over all recorded data in the character generator. This ensures the production assistant of accuracy and informs the assistant director of character generator copy available.

Reviewing the character generator recorded copy (AD 6) The assistant director reviews all recorded character generator copy to check the production assistant for accuracy and to be informed of the character generator copy available for the production.

Alerting the director when ready (PA 7) The production assistant lets the director know when the character generator copy is recorded, stored in memory, checked, and ready.

Organizing the studio set for readiness and checking props on spike marks (F 4) The floor director pays constant attention to changes on the studio set. With talent coming and going and the movement of the studio production crew, the set and props need reorganizing before production begins. During rehearsal(s), the placement of set properties and talent were spiked for ease in returning to the same lighted spot during subsequent production.

Setting levels for playback audio cartridge sources (A 6) The audio director needs to play back each audio cartridge source to set gain levels and equalization and tone settings for each source. For example, a possible audio playback cartridge needing an audio level set is the opening theme music for the program.

Checking and recuing all prerecorded audio sources (A 7) The audio director checks and then recues all prerecorded audio sources controlled from the audio control board.

Getting dressed for the program and applying make-up (T 7) After the talent has been over the script and marked it for reading and has met the guests for the program, the talent retires to a dressing room to get dressed with on-air wardrobe and put on make-up.

Checking the network intercom connections (A 8) The audio director checks the network intercom connections that will be necessary to the audio director during production. The normal connections that the audio director will need are to the director, assistant director, and, perhaps, technical director.

Reporting to the studio set and maintaining spike marks (T 8) The talent reports to the floor director and the studio set when dressed and made up. Spike marks on the set are part of the program design and are used for consistency in production. The talent should maintain the designated spike mark positions while working on the set.

Checking teleprompter monitors for reading ease and light reflections (T 9) The talent practices reading the teleprompter for reading ease as well as checking for annoying light reflections or glare on the prompter monitors.

Resetting countdown timer(s) and checking stop watch(es) or counters for front, back, and segment times during production (AD 7) The assistant director sets all timing devices in the control room to measure the front time of the program (i.e., from 00:00 to 28:30), back time (i.e., from 28:30 to 00:00), and segment times (i.e., the individual times of B-rolled video sources).

Patching and testing audio foldback sound to the studio (A 9) The audio director patches the audio foldback sound to the studio. The audio foldback sound will allow the studio crew to hear all of the audio program line from the audio control board. This permits the crew to hear audio out-cues during production. The foldback sound has to be tested for gain level to avoid feedback. The teleprompter operator also relies on foldback to follow the talent reading voice.

Calling for studio talent microphone checks and setting levels for each (A 10) With foldback in working order, the audio director calls into the studio for talent microphone checks. This entails asking talent to use the microphone naturally and read some copy into it until the audio director sets gain, equalization, and tone levels for each talent microphone to be used during production.

Making a microphone level check (T 10) The talent and guest(s) respond to the audio director's call for a microphone level check by counting from one to ten slowly at a normal speaking level. Talent and guest(s) should continue to count until the audio director announces that the gain levels are set for each individual on the studio set.

Checking on the talent and guest(s), calling them to the studio and set when necessary, and monitoring their readiness (F 5) The floor director keeps a constant check on the talent, and on their stages of necessary checks from microphone setting to make-up. The floor director monitors talent readiness until production time. Talent and guest(s) may have to be summoned from dressing rooms and make-up to the studio and their places on the set.

Checking intercom network connections (F 6) The floor director checks all intercom network connections needed by the floor director to be in communication from

the studio to the control room during production. The most important intercom connection for the floor director is to the director; in addition, the floor director should be in intercom connection with the assistant director.

Having the floor director check make-up under studio set lights (T 11) Before giving a ready signal, the talent has the floor director check the talent's make-up under set lighting for shine and repair it by powdering.

Alerting the floor director when ready (T 12) The talent alerts the floor director when ready to begin production.

Checking on camera operators and monitoring their readiness (F 7) As the floor director is the director's "other self" in the studio, the floor director is responsible for constantly checking on the readiness of the camera operators before production begins. This includes noting camera operators' absence from the studio for restroom purposes.

Checking on lighting, light instruments, and lighting pattern working order (F 8) Because the floor director is constantly aware of studio details before and during production, one area of detail checking is all phases of studio lighting. Lighting bulbs can go out at any moment. Awareness of the lighting pattern on the set and aimed instruments is a part of the floor director's responsibilities.

Checking audio foldback in the studio (F 9) The floor director keeps a constant check before production for the proper operation and gain level of the audio sound foldback in the studio.

Setting audio levels for each playback B-roll video source(s) (A 11) While the technical director and video-tape recorder operator are checking each B-roll video source playback for video levels, the audio director takes the opportunity of the video playback to set audio levels for each B-roll video source. Setting audio levels involves recording the gain level, equalization, and tone settings for each video. These levels and settings will have to be recorded where they can be preset again before each B-roll video source plays during production.

Alerting the director when ready (A 12) When all audio production checks have been made, the audio director should signal the director that all audio sources are ready for production.

Making make-up checks on the talent and repairing powdering when necessary (F 10) The floor director must keep a constant visual check on the make-up of the talent. Pressure and waiting can create talent perspiration and oils can overpower make-up to cause facial shining. The floor director repairs talent make-up with powder whenever it is needed.

Alerting the director when the studio is ready (F 11) The floor director is the best positioned crew member to indicate to the director and the control room the state of readiness of the studio crew and talent.

Awaiting a "ready" cue from production personnel: audio director, camera operators, lighting director, production assistant, technical director, floor director, talent, video engineer, and videotape recorder operator (D 8) The director comes to a moment in production preparation when other production crew and talent have to indicate their readiness to begin. It is better if the director does not have to page all crew to check on their readiness; rather, the crew should alert the director when they are ready. (See the director's checklist form.)

Calling a stand-by cue to all studio, control room, and master control production crew (D 9) The director cues all production crew by calling a stand-by as a signal that the production is about to begin. This alerts all crew in the studio, control room, and master control areas.

Preparing to follow the format/rundown sheet for the director (AD 8) The assistant director prepares to follow the program's format/rundown sheet as a stand-by call is announced. This generally means that the assistant director uses a finger or pencil to point to the area of the format/rundown sheet where the production is at any moment.

Communicating the director's commands to studio personnel (F 12) The floor director is responsible for relaying all of the director's commands to the studio personnel out loud before production begins and by hand signals after production has begun.

Calling and maintaining readiness in the studio (F 13) The floor director relays the stand-by cue to the studio personnel and maintains crew attention and readiness until the director advances to the videotape rolling and the program opening.

Standing by with the floor director's call (T 13) The talent take a stand-by position as the floor director relays the director's call for a stand-by for studio production.

Attending to the floor director for the opening cue to begin (TO 8) The prompter operator pays attention to the floor director for the cue from the director to begin running the teleprompter script for the talent.

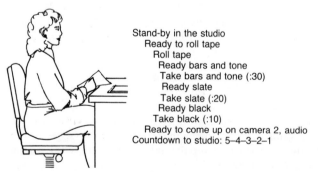

Stand-by in the studio
Ready to roll tape
Roll tape
Ready bars and tone
Take bars and tone (:30)
Ready slate
Take slate (:20)
Ready black
Take black (:10)
Ready to come up on camera 2, audio
Countdown to studio: 5–4–3–2–1

FIGURE 2–19
The director's beginning commands. The director begins the program's videotaping session with special commands that signal the start of the videotape, ready the crew, record the academy leader, and begin the opening of the program.

Listening for the director's call for lighting cues and changes (LD 8) The lighting director listens closely for any cues from the director to begin or make any lighting changes. A production value of the program may involve bringing studio set lights up or down on cue.

Calling to the videotape recorder operator a "ready to roll tape" and a cue to "roll videotape" (D 10) When the director is ready to begin production or real clock time for telecast has arrived, the director cues the beginning of videotape recording by calling for a "ready to roll tape." The director awaits the videotape recorder operator's response that the tape is ready. The director then calls for the videotape to begin rolling.

Responding to the director's call to ready the videotape deck and to roll the videotape by readying the videotape deck and then beginning to operate the videotape deck (VTRO 10) The videotape recorder operator stands by by readying the videotape deck being used for recording the program, and rolling the videotape—actually operating the deck—when the director calls to ready to roll tape and then to roll the videotape.

Awaiting clock time and counting down final seconds to the program opening (D 11) The director watches the clock time for program videotaping start time at the director's discretion and counts down the remaining seconds to the start of the program production. If the program is being telecast live, the production starting time is real clock time.

Awaiting the director's opening cues (A 13) The audio director awaits the director's opening cues, which may involve audio control sources.

Reading aloud the clock and timer countdowns to the opening of the program production and other time cues during production (AD 9) The assistant director watches all clocks and timers and reads countdown times loudly for all to hear. The assistant director begins this service for the opening of the program and continues throughout the production to the closing time.

Listening and responding to the director's commands (TD 8) The technical director is responsible for listening carefully to all of the director's commands during the program production and responding with the video source changes.

Switching appropriate video sources (TD 9) The technical director faithfully responds to all of the director's commands to the technical director by appropriately changing the video sources through the switcher.

Repeating all countdowns to the studio to a 2-second call (F 14) The floor director repeats all of the director's countdowns to the studio by counting aloud down to the 2-second count. The remaining seconds are counted silently by all studio production crew so that unwanted sounds are not picked up by the studio microphones.

Changing and keeping the character generator screen text current for succeeding use (PA 8) The production assistant should always keep the character generator copy screen page current, ready for the next listed page. Advancing the next page should be done only after the technical director removes the previous screen page from the program line.

Signaling to the talent which cameras are "on" (F 15) The floor director signals to the talent whenever a camera change is made by the director by indicating which camera to change to and which camera is "on." The floor director accomplishes this by using hand signals.

Beginning with the floor director's signal from the director to begin and the camera tally light goes on (T 14) The talent begins ad-libbing or reading the script copy when the floor director signals the director's cue to begin. Affirming that signal to begin is the tally light operation on the opening camera.

Directing the format/rundown sheet and "taking" all formatted video and audio sources (D 12) Having begun the program's opening, the director continues by following the script with the assistance of the assistant director. All B-roll video and audio sources indicated on the format/rundown sheet are "taken" by the director when noted.

Readying camera shots and calling a "take" to the technical director (D 13) The director follows control room procedure with studio crew and control room crew by readying each camera shot (or prerecorded video or character generator screen copy) and calling the "take" as each is to be switched into the program line by the technical director.

Following the director's calls during the program production (A 14) The audio director now follows, as does the technical director for video sources, all cues referring to audio sources into the program during production.

Maintaining communication between the director and the studio (F 16) The floor director maintains two-way communication between the director and the studio throughout the production.

Maintaining ready positions until the director calls for a new set-up (CO 12) Camera operators keep their defined and readied camera shots (i.e., framing) in position until the director calls for a new camera shot set-up.

Advancing the character generator screen copy when the technical director clears the previous matte from the program line (PA 9) The production assistant advances the character generator screen copy as previous screen pages are used and matted into the program. The production assistant changes and previews succeeding copy when the technical director has removed any previous matte copy from the program line. This procedure is used unless character generator copy must change on screen while on the program line.

Following the talent carefully and keeping the script copy at the desired screen height (TO 9) The tele-prompter operator follows the talent script content reading very carefully over the studio foldback and keeps the script copy at the desired reading height for the talent.

Operating and advancing or monitoring the telecine during production (TC 8) The telecine operator either operates and advances film sources in the telecine throughout program production or monitors the telecine as the assistant director operates and advances film sources by remote control from the control room.

Operating and advancing the telecine as needed or communicating the cue to operate and advance the telecine (AD 10) The assistant director either operates and advances the telecine film sources by remote control or communicates the cues to operate and advance the telecine to the telecine operator during production.

Monitoring the studio set and the talent over the control room monitors during videotaping (LD 9) The lighting director constantly monitors the studio set and the talent over the control room monitors for any lighting problems. Some lighting problems might be corrected by adjusting light intensity during videotaping. The lighting director notes other changes to be made before the next videotaping session.

Reading out loud expected out-cues to all B-roll video and audio sources (AD 11) The assistant director loudly reads expected out-cues to all B-roll video and audio sources into the program. Out-cues are the final few words of copy or visual images at the end of a prerecorded video insert. Knowing the expected out-cues permits crew members to anticipate the end of the video and effect the next changes in the program.

Keeping close tabs on all timed prerecorded video sources (AD 12) During the B-roll of all prerecorded video sources, the assistant director keeps accurate time with a stop watch. All prerecorded times usually from first audio (or first video) to final audio (or final video) are reported by the producer on the format/rundown sheet.

Operating videotape playback decks by remote control or readying the videotape playback sources for operation (AD 13) The assistant director operates the videotape playback decks by remote control if they are controlled from the control room. If the videotape recorder operator operates the playback decks manually, the assistant director readies the videotape playback sources for operation. A preroll time of 3 to 5 seconds is anticipated in some production operations. The director calls the take to the technical director.

Readying all character generator screen copy (AD 14) The assistant director readies all character generator screen copy for insertion into the program. Notation for character generator copy insertion is among the notations on the format/rundown sheet.

Communicating to the talent during commercial breaks any changes from the director or the producer (F 17) The floor director takes the opportunity during commercial breaks to communicate to the talent any changes or messages from the director or the producer.

Repairing talent make-up during commercial breaks (F 18) The floor director takes commercial break time to check and powder the talent's make-up to diminish any shine.

Communicating to the director any information from the studio or studio crew (F 19) The floor director relays any information (e.g., questions) from the studio crew to the director.

Listening to and following the director's calls during production (CO 13) The camera operators listen carefully to and follow all of the director's calls regarding their cameras throughout the program production.

Standing by for any changes or corrections from the telecine film sources during the program and reloading sources if necessary (TC 9) The telecine operator, whether operating the telecine manually or monitoring the remote control use of the telecine, stands by for any changes or corrections that may be needed from the telecine film sources during the program production. When 35mm slides are being used in production, the necessity to reload the telecine's slide drums is always a possibility.

Following the format/rundown sheet for the program unit for production (T 15) The talent follows closely the producer's format/rundown sheet for the program being produced. Talent may bring a copy of the format/rundown sheet on the set. In some operations, the format/rundown sheet is presented to the talent over the studio teleprompter.

Following the floor director's communication during production (T 16) The talent follows any communication from the floor director, whether the commands are given verbally during breaks in production or by hand signals during videotaping.

Repairing or having repairs made to make-up during commercial breaks (T 17) During the stress of on-air demands as well as the heat generated from studio lighting, talent make-up will need constant repair during program production. The talent may repair the talent's own make-up by powdering or may be assisted by the floor director. It is the floor director who keeps constant vigil on the need for talent make-up repair. Powdering repairs to make-up are made during commercial breaks from studio production.

Monitoring playback and record videotape decks during production (VTRO 11) The videotape recorder operator constantly monitors all videotape recording and playback decks during videotape production.

Monitoring the video light levels of cameras during production (VEG 6) The video engineer monitors the video light levels of all cameras during the program production. When light levels on the set and talent change, lens apertures are changed accordingly.

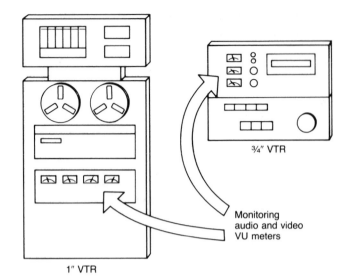

FIGURE 2–20
Monitoring audio and video levels. The videotape recorder operator has to monitor the VU meters of videotape decks for audio and video signals during production. Loss or absence of a signal means a problem for the production.

Alerting the director to any soft focused cameras during production (VEG 7) The video engineer also monitors the cameras for any soft focused cameras and alerts the director to pass the information along to the offending camera operator for fine focusing change.

Conferring with the producer for any program content or format decisions (D 14) The director confers with the producer during the program production on any questions that arise regarding the program's content or format.

Conferring with the director during production on program content and format decisions (P 8) The producer evaluates the time remaining in the program and makes any content decisions (e.g., to delete some content in the event the program is running long or to add some pad content if it is running short) and conveys those decisions to the director.

Closing the program production (D 15) The director brings the program production to a close following real clock time or program front or back time.

Announcing any postproduction needs to the program production (D 16) The director decides, with the counsel of the producer, whether to make any postproduction changes or corrections to the program videotape recording. This would be a consideration only if the program is a tape delayed telecast or even if postproduction is possible and necessary. The director announces a decision to the production crew. The director calls either a program wrap (a *wrap* means that the program videotaping is complete), a studio strike (in a *studio strike*, the studio, control room, and master control personnel can shut down equipment, videotape(s), and studio set, and the talent can leave the studio and remove make-up), or postproduction.

Preparing any postproduction needs from the production crew or assisting the program wrap (AD 15) The assistant director reacts to the director's call for postproduction by activating subordinate crew to respond or assisting in the call for a program wrap and studio strike.

Preparing for any postproduction needs or stopping down the switcher at the director's call for a wrap (TD 10) The technical director either prepares to continue technical direction in postproduction or stops down the switcher at the director's call for a program wrap and studio strike.

Preparing for any postproduction needs or turning off the character generator at the call for a program wrap (PA 10) The production assistant either prepares to continue character generator control during postproduction or turns the character generator off at the call for a program wrap.

Preparing for any postproduction needs or striking the audio set-up at the call for a wrap (A 15) The audio director either prepares to contribute audio production elements if needed in postproduction or strikes the audio set-up at the call for a program wrap and studio strike.

Relaying the director's call for a hold in studio positions pending a call for postproduction or a program wrap and studio strike (F 20) The floor director relays the director's call to hold studio positions pending a decision to do postproduction involving the studio crew or that the production is complete and the call is for a program wrap and a studio strike.

Holding studio positions pending a decision to do studio postproduction work or striking the cameras at a program wrap (CO 14) Camera operators either hold their positions pending the director's decision to do some postproduction of the program that may involve the studio cameras or begin to strike the cameras at the director's call for a program wrap.

Holding prompter position pending the director's decision to do studio postproduction work involving the script or beginning to strike the teleprompter at the call to wrap (TO 10) The prompter operator either holds the studio position pending the director's decision to do some postproduction on the program that involves the script or begins to strike the teleprompter equipment at the call for a program wrap.

Holding the telecine operation pending the director's decision to do postproduction on the program or beginning to strike the telecine and film sources at the call to wrap (TC 10) The telecine operator either holds at the telecine awaiting the director's decision to do postproduction on the program that might involve the film sources or prepares to strike the telecine and film sources.

Holding studio positions pending the director's decision to do postproduction on the program involving the talent or preparing for the program wrap (T 18) The talent hold their studio positions at the floor director's command pending the director's decision to do postproduction on the program involving the talent or prepare for the program wrap and studio strike call.

Preparing for any postproduction needs involving lighting or beginning to strike studio lighting at the director's call for a program wrap (LD 10) The lighting director prepares to contribute to postproduction if lighting needs are involved or begins to strike studio lighting with the call for a program wrap and studio strike.

Preparing for any videotape recording postproduction needs for which the director may call or beginning to strike the videotape and shut down the videotape decks (VTRO 12) The videotape recorder operator will be involved in any postproduction on the program. The videotape recorder operator awaits the director's call. At a program wrap and studio strike call the videotape recorder operator begins to shut down the videotape decks.

Preparing for postproduction needs that the director may call for requiring studio cameras or beginning to strike the cameras by capping the lenses (VEG 8) The video engineer prepares for the director's call to do postproduction on the program involving the studio cameras or begins to strike the cameras and the video control area by capping the lenses of the cameras. The studio cameras are then turned off electronically.

Overseeing the studio strike in the control room (AD 16) The assistant director oversees the studio strike in the control area. This entails collecting forms and logs from control room personnel that will become part of the program history and will become a point of reference for future productions of the program. Any papers important to the director are collected and saved. The assistant director oversees other studio strike positions while the director is in a critique session with the producer and the talent.

Overseeing the complete studio strike in the studio (F 21) The floor director oversees the studio strike in the studio area of production. This includes cameras, lighting, and set and properties storage.

Shutting down the production switcher with a wrap and studio strike call (TD 11) The technical director shuts down the production switcher at the director's call for a program wrap and studio strike. This entails putting video sources into a video black mode and collecting any notes on the production format/rundown sheet the technical director made for feedback during the critique session and production meeting.

Preparing postproduction needs or closing down the audio control panel with a program wrap and studio strike call (A 15) The audio director prepares for postproduction needs required from the audio portion of the program or closes down the audio control board when the director calls for a program wrap and studio strike. This entails unpatching audio sources and rewinding audio tapes and cartridges for storage.

Rewinding videotapes at a program wrap call and labeling all videotapes and videotape storage cases (VTRO 13) The videotape recorder operator strikes the videotape decks by rewinding all videotape source tapes and the master videotape and by labeling the videotapes and the videotape storage cases.

Securing guest release signatures (P 9) After a program wrap and studio strike, the producer secures any remaining talent release signatures from guest(s) on the program. The release will permit rerun and promotional use of the guest(s) beyond the program just videotaped.

Calling for and meeting with the producer and talent in a program critique session (D 17) The director takes studio strike time to call and meet with the producer and the talent for a brief critique session. The director meets with the producer and the talent alone in deference to the producer and the talent and their respect and credibility. The three should handle self criticism and crew criticism as a means to improving the program in succeeding productions. These critique sessions should continue after subsequent productions until the producer and director sense that the program production is on track and that they have achieved what they want for the program. The director should take notes at this meeting of things to be brought up before the whole crew during their critique session. The videotape of the program may or may not be viewed during this session.

Calling for and meeting with the director and talent for a program critique session (P 10) The producer may call for and meet with the director and talent before a production crew critique session. This is the opportunity for the producer to give feedback to both the director and the talent. Content from this critique session forms the basis of criticism during the crew critique session. The producer may wish to view the videotape of the program as part of this session.

Meeting with the producer and the director for a critique of the program (T 19) The talent meets with the producer and the director in a closed critique session of the program just produced. This is an opportunity for personal criticism of the talent's performance as well as an opportunity for the talent to offer feedback about suggested changes to the format, production values, and the talent's performance.

Calling for and meeting with the entire production crew for a critique session and production meeting (D 18) The director calls for a critique session with the entire production crew after the studio strike. This session serves as a production meeting for future productions of the program. The director may have the crew view the videotape of the program. The director conveys to the crew the producer's and talent's criticisms and suggested changes. This allows for improving performances on future

programs. The director also solicits feedback from the crew.

Calling for and meeting with the entire production crew for a critique session and production meeting (P 11) The producer may call for a critique session and meet with the entire production crew for a postvideotaping critique of the production. This session may also serve as a production meeting for future productions. If the producer does not call the session, the producer will meet with the crew during the meeting called by the director. Both the producer and the director offer feedback to the crew on their performance and suggest changes to future program productions.

Meeting with the producer and director for a post-videotaping critique session and production meeting for future productions (AD 17) The assistant director meets with the producer and director for a postvideotaping critique session of the program just completed. The crew may be asked to view the videotape of the program.

This meeting also serves as a production meeting for future program productions. Each crew member should take notes on any relevant criticism. Crew members should also make suggestions for improving future productions.

Meeting with the producer and director for a post-videotaping critique session and production meeting for future productions (F 22) The floor director meets with the producer and director for a postvideotaping critique session of the program just completed. The crew may be asked to view the videotape of the program.

This meeting also serves as a production meeting for future program productions. Each crew member should take notes on any relevant criticism. Crew members should also make suggestions for improving future productions.

Meeting with the producer and director for a post-videotaping critique session and production meeting for future productions (TD 12) The technical director meets with the producer and director for a postvideotaping critique session of the program just completed. The crew may be asked to view the videotape of the program.

This meeting also serves as a production meeting for future program productions. Each crew member should take notes on any relevant criticism. Crew members should also make suggestions for improving future productions.

Meeting with the producer and director for a post-videotaping critique session and production meeting for future productions (CO 15) The camera operators meet with the producer and director for a postvideotaping critique session of the program just completed. The crew may be asked to view the videotape of the program.

This meeting also serves as a production meeting for future program productions. Each crew member should take notes on any relevant criticism. Crew members should also make suggestions for improving future productions.

Meeting with the producer and director for a post-videotaping critique session and production meeting for future productions (A 16) The audio director meets with the producer and director for a postvideotaping critique session of the program just completed. The crew may be asked to view the videotape of the program.

This meeting also serves as a production meeting for future program productions. Each crew member should take notes on any relevant criticism. Crew members should also make suggestions for improving future productions.

Meeting with the producer and director for a post-videotaping critique session and production meeting for future productions (LD 11) The lighting director meets with the producer and director for a postvideotaping critique session of the program just completed. The crew may be asked to view the videotape of the program.

This meeting also serves as a production meeting for future program productions. Each crew member should take notes on any relevant criticism. Crew members should also make suggestions for improving future productions.

Meeting with the producer and director for a post-videotaping critique session and production meeting for future productions (PA 11) The production assistant meets with the producer and director for a postvideotaping critique session of the program just completed. The crew may be asked to view the videotape of the program.

This meeting also serves as a production meeting for future program productions. Each crew member should take notes on any relevant criticism. Crew members should also make suggestions for improving future productions.

Meeting with the producer and director for a post-videotaping critique session and production meeting for future productions (TO 11) The teleprompter operator meets with the producer and director for a postvideotaping critique session of the program just completed. The crew may be asked to view the videotape of the program.

This meeting also serves as a production meeting for future program productions. Each crew member should take notes on any relevant criticism. Crew members should also make suggestions for improving future productions.

Meeting with the producer and director for a post-videotaping critique session and production meeting for future productions (TC 11) The telecine operator meets with the producer and director for a postvideotaping critique session of the program just completed. The crew may be asked to view the videotape of the program.

This meeting also serves as a production meeting for future program productions. Each crew member should take notes on any relevant criticism. Crew members should also make suggestions for improving future productions.

Meeting with the producer and director for a post-videotaping critique session and production meeting for future productions (VTRO 14) The videotape recorder operator meets with the producer and director for a postvideotaping critique session of the program just completed. The crew may be asked to view the videotape of the program.

This meeting also serves as a production meeting for future program productions. Each crew member should

take notes on any relevant criticism. Crew members should also make suggestions for improving future productions.

Meeting with the producer and director for a post-videotaping critique session and production meeting for future productions (VEG 9) The video engineer meets with the producer and director for a postvideotaping critique session of the program just completed. The crew may be asked to view the videotape of the program.

This meeting also serves as a production meeting for future program productions. Each crew member should take notes on any relevant criticism. Crew members should also make suggestions for improving future productions.

THE POSTPRODUCTION PROCESS

If the talk show/entertainment program production just completed was telecast live, there is little reason to consider postproduction work on the program. However, if the talk show/entertainment program is to be telecast later, some postproduction may be done. The individuals who have the authority to choose to do postproduction on the program are either the producer or the director.

The question of postproduction is a subjective one for most producers and directors. But there are production problems that warrant some consideration of redoing or correcting. Some of the most common reasons for engaging in postproduction while the talent and production crew are still in place include a spelling error in character generator copy, completely erroneous character generator copy, missing character generator copy, a slip of the tongue by the talent, a B-roll video problem, bad microphone, studio gaffe (e.g., unwanted noise), or wrong audio cartridge. Most of these errors or problems can be corrected in a few moments of recuing record videotape, reestablishing the video or audio problem source, activating the necessary production crew, and rolling the videotape as soon as production elements are ready.

For major program production problems, a simple solution is to redo a unit of the program from commercial break to commercial break. This may be a workable solution when the problem encompasses a complete section of the program involving a guest. Redoing the closing of the program, including theme music and credits, provides an opportunity to lengthen or shorten the program depending on the particular time problem.

• Personnel

Only two staff personnel have new roles in any talk show/entertainment program postproduction: the producer and the director.

Producer (P) The producer may take some responsibility for any problems or errors in the program that are at fault in the producing stage of the production. Because the producer is responsible for getting all assigned producing work done, the producer can use that authority to require postproduction work on the program.

Director (D) The director may take responsibility for problems or mistakes that were caused by production crew under the director's supervision. The director has the authority to decide to do postproduction work on the talk show/entertainment program.

All other production crew members All remaining production crew members are the same as those described at the production stage of the program. Roles and responsibilities remain identical to those performed during production.

- **Postproduction Stages**

Assuming a decision-making role to add to or redo those elements of the program that involve producing errors or problems (P 1) The producer may decide that some elements of the program involved errors or problems in production. The producer takes responsibility for producing errors or problems and has the director begin postproduction with those areas of production involved in correcting and redoing portions of the program.

Communicating those elements of the producing stage of the program that will become a part of the postproduction process (P 2) The producer tells the director which parts of the program are producing errors or problems and will become part of the required postproduction.

Continuing as in the production stage of the program (P 3) The producer continues during postproduction in the role as defined for the producer in the production process.

Assuming authority and responsibility and a decision-making role to add to or redo elements of the program that involve studio production errors or problems and communicating these to the producer (D 1) The director may take the authority, responsibility, and decision-making role to correct and redo elements of the program that involved studio production errors or problems. The director communicates these intentions to the producer.

Alerting the specific production crew members who will be involved in postproduction (D 2) The director informs those production crew members who will be involved in postproduction. For example, if postproduction involves only control room personnel (e.g., the technical director must add character generator copy matte, which will involve the production assistant), studio personnel are given a wrap call.

Continuing as in the production stage of the program (D 3) The director continues postproduction in the role the director had in the production stage of the program.

Readying those crew members who will be involved in postproduction work on the program (AD 1) The assistant director readies those production crew members who will be involved in the postproduction stage of the program.

Continuing as in the production stage of the program (AD 2) The assistant director continues in the role defined for the assistant director at the production stage of the program.

Preparing to add or redo those elements of the program in postproduction that involve the production switcher (TD 1) The technical director prepares to add or redo those elements of the program in postproduction that involve the production switcher.

Communicating to the videotape recorder operator what video sources will be involved in postproduction (TD 2) The technical director communicates to the videotape recorder operator those video sources, if any, that will be involved in the postproduction stage of the program.

Continuing as in the production stage of the program (TD 3) The technical director continues in the role defined for the technical director at the production stage of the program.

Preparing to ready those elements of the character generator that will be involved in postproduction (PA 1) The production assistant prepares to ready any character generator copy that will be involved in the postproduction of the program.

Continuing as in the production stage of the program (PA 2) The production assistant continues in the role defined for the production assistant at the production stage of the program.

Preparing to ready those audio sources that will be involved in postproduction (A 1) The audio director prepares to ready any audio sources for which the audio director will be responsible during postproduction.

Continuing as in the production stage of the program (A 2) The audio director continues in the role defined for the floor director at the production stage of the program production.

Preparing to ready and maintain control of those elements in the studio that will be involved in postproduction (F 1) The floor director must keep studio personnel informed, get them ready, and maintain readiness for whatever elements, if any, of the program involve the studio personnel in postproduction.

Continuing as in the production stage of the program (F 2) The floor director assumes the role defined for the floor director at the production stage of the program.

Preparing to ready the studio cameras that will be involved in postproduction for the program (CO 1) The camera operators prepare to ready themselves and their cameras for whatever, if any, elements of the studio cameras are required in postproduction.

Continuing as in the production stage of the program (CO 2) The camera operators continue in the role defined for them at the production stage of the program.

Preparing to ready the teleprompter script for postproduction (TO 1) The teleprompter operator prepares to ready the script for use in postproduction if it is necessary.

Continuing as in the production stage of the program (TO 2) The teleprompter operator continues in the role defined for the teleprompter operator and the use of the script during the production stage of the program.

Preparing to ready the film sources in the telecine for postproduction (TC 1) The telecine operator prepares to ready whatever film sources at the telecine may be required in the postproduction of the program.

Continuing as in the production stage of the program (TC 2) The telecine operator continues in the role defined for the telecine operator at the production stage of the program.

Preparing to redo any studio video and script copy for postproduction (T 1) The talent in the studio prepares to redo any studio video or script copy if it is required in postproduction.

Continuing as in the production stage of the program (T 2) The talent continues in the role defined for the talent at the production stage of the program.

Readying those studio lighting elements that may be involved in the postproduction of the program (LD 1) The lighting director readies those studio lighting elements that may be involved in the postproduction of the program.

Continuing as in the production stage of the program (LD 2) The lighting director continues in the role defined for the lighting director at the production stage of the program.

Readying the videotape decks for postproduction (VTRO 1) The videotape recorder operator readies those playback and record videotape decks that may be involved in postproduction. At the least, the videotape recorder operator will have to cue up the record deck and oversee the recording of postproduction elements.

Continuing as in the production stage of the program (VTRO 2) The videotape recorder operator continues during postproduction in the role defined for the videotape recorder operator in the production stage of the program.

Readying the cameras and video levels for postproduction (VEG 1) The video engineer readies the cameras and their video levels if the studio cameras are involved in postproduction.

Continuing as in the production stage of the program (VEG 2) The video engineer continues as in the production stage of the program.

Chapter 3

Studio Production Organizing Forms

There is a diversity and breadth of roles and task responsibilities in television studio talk show/entertainment program producing and production. This diversity and breadth warrant some technique within which role and task responsibility of personnel can be successfully met. It is frequently said in television production that the success of a production is a function of the extent and degree of preproduction.

Organizing forms are presented in this chapter for almost all information gathering and task preparation stages required for talk show/ entertainment program preproduction and production. The majority of the forms serve to design and order talk show/entertainment program origination and producing tasks. The remaining forms help to prepare for the actual studio production of the program. Included are forms that were designed to assist in the development and design of the program and in the development of talent from audition through rehearsal(s) and telecast. As with many resources in a creative and technological medium, not all forms will be equally functional. These forms should be used when they facilitate the tasks for which they were created. They should not become ends in themselves. Forms that serve the production should be used and perhaps adapted to the requirements of a particular program or studio production facility. Others may be needed and may serve a one time only function. Still others may not be required and should be overlooked.

The forms presented here are designed to be used by producing and production personnel for particular role accomplishment. Those roles are listed in the upper portions of the respective forms. These forms can be removed or photocopied. Note that each form's structure and function are detailed in Chapter 4.

PROGRAM PROPOSAL
MULTIPLE CAMERA VIDEO TALK SHOW/ENTERTAINMENT PROGRAM PRODUCTION

Producer: Date: /   /   Page   of

Proposed Program Title:
Rationale:

Proposed Program Length: :
Proposed Number of Breaks/Commercials: Break Length:

Proposed Network/Station/Production Facility: Studio Production Hours:
Production Requirements: Postproduction Hours:

Production Crew Requirements:

Proposed Telecast Time:
    Day: Time: :   AM/PM
Alternate Time(s):
    Day: Time: :   AM/PM

Style/Format of Proposed Program:

Proposed/Suggested Sponsorship:

ATTACHED
- ☐ Program Treatment   ☐ Preproduction Script   ☐ Set Design
- ☐ Program Budget   ☐ Program Format   ☐ _____

PROGRAM TREATMENT
MULTIPLE CAMERA VIDEO TALK SHOW/ENTERTAINMENT PROGRAM PRODUCTION

Producer:

Date: / /

Program Title:

Program Length: :

Page of

Program Goals and Objectives:

Target Audience:

Program Description:

Production Values:

Production Statement:

PREPRODUCTION SCRIPT
MULTIPLE CAMERA VIDEO TALK SHOW/ENTERTAINMENT PROGRAM PRODUCTION

Producer:

Program Title:

Date: /   /

Page   of

VIDEO	AUDIO

VIDEO	AUDIO

PRODUCTION BUDGET
MULTIPLE CAMERA VIDEO TALK SHOW/ENTERTAINMENT PROGRAM PRODUCTION

Producer:

Director:

Date: / /

Program Title:

Length: :

Page   of

No. Preproduction Days: ☐ Hours: ☐ First Production Date: / /

No. Studio Shoot Days: ☐ Hours: ☐ No. Programs in Series: ☐

No. Postproduction Days: ☐ Hours: ☐

SUMMARY OF PRODUCTION COSTS	ESTIMATED	ACTUAL
1. Rights and Clearances		
2. Producer, Staff, and Expenses		
3. Director, Staff, and Expenses		
4. Talent		
5. Benefits		
6. Production Facility		
7. Production Staff		
8. Cameras, Videotape Recording, Video Engineering		
9. Set Design, Construction, Decoration, Properties		
10. Set Lighting		
11. Audio Production		
12. Wardrobe, Make-up, and Hairstyling		
13. Videotape Stock		
14. Postproduction Editing		
15. Music		
16. Subtotal		
17. Contingency		
Grand Total		

COMMENTS

RIGHTS AND CLEARANCES		ESTIMATED	ACTUAL
1. Rights Purchased			
2. Title and Logo Trademark			
3. Other Rights			
4. Music Clearances			
5.			
	Subtotal		

PRODUCER AND STAFF

CREW	ESTIMATED				ACTUAL			
	Days	Rate	O/T Hrs	Total	Days	Rate	O/T Hrs	Total
6. Producer								
7. Preproduction								
8. Production								
9. Postproduction								
10.								
11. Secretary No. ( )								
12.								
13. Producer Supplies								
14. Photocopying								
15. Telephone								
16. Postage								
17. Travel Expenses								
18. Per Diem								
19. Miscellaneous								
20.								
Subtotal								

DIRECTOR AND STAFF

CREW	ESTIMATED				ACTUAL			
	Days	Rate	O/T Hrs	Total	Days	Rate	O/T Hrs	Total
21. Director								
22. Preproduction								
23. Production								
24. Postproduction								
25. Assistant Director								
26. Preproduction								
27. Production								
28. Postproduction								
29.								
30. Secretary No. ( )								
31.								
32. Director's Supplies								
33. Photocopying								
34. Telephone								
35. Postage								
36. Travel Expenses								
37. Per Diem								
38. Expenses								
39. Miscellaneous								
40.								
Subtotal								

TALENT

DESCRIPTION	ESTIMATED				ACTUAL			
	Days	Rate	O/T Hrs	Total	Days	Rate	O/T Hrs	Total
41. Talent (Contract)								
42. Host/Hostess								
43. Moderator								
44. Preproduction								
45. Production								
46. Postproduction								
47. Talent (Freelance)								
48. Host/Hostess								
49. Moderator								
50. Preproduction								
51. Production								
52. Postproduction								
53.								
54. Specialty Acts								
55.								
56. Guest								
57. Reimbursements								
58. Travel								
59. Hotel								
60. Extra Talent								
61.								
	Subtotal							

BENEFITS

DESCRIPTION	TOTAL
62. Insurance Coverage	
63. Health Plan	
64. Welfare Plan	
65. Taxes (FICA, etc.)	
66. Equity/Guild/Union Costs	
Subtotal	

PRODUCTION FACILITY

SPACE	ESTIMATED				ACTUAL			
	Days	Rate	O/T Hrs	Total	Days	Rate	O/T Hrs	Total
67. Production Studio								
68. Studio Camera								
69. Studio Camera								
70. Studio Camera								
71. Teleprompter								
72. Floor Monitor								
73. Floor Monitor								
74.								
75. Control Room								
76. Production Switcher								
77. Digital Video Effects								
78. Still Store								
79.								

PRODUCTION FACILITY (Con't)

SPACE	ESTIMATED				ACTUAL			
	Days	Rate	O/T Hrs	Total	Days	Rate	O/T Hrs	Total
80. Intercom Network								
81.								
82. Character Generator								
83.								
84. Audio Control Board								
85. Cartridge Playback								
86. Cassette Playback								
87. Reel-to-Reel Playback								
88. Turntable								
89. Compact Disc Player								
90. Studio Foldback								
91.								
92. Master Control								
93. Record Deck No.( )								
94. Playback Deck No.( )								
95.								
96. Telecine								
97. 16mm								
98. 35mm								
99. Other								
100.								
101. Dressing Rooms								
102. Make-Up Facility								
103. Green Room								
104. Other								
	Subtotal							

PRODUCTION STAFF

SPACE	ESTIMATED				ACTUAL			
	Days	Rate	O/T Hrs	Total	Days	Rate	O/T Hrs	Total
105. Technical Director								
106. Preproduction								
107. Production								
108. Postproduction								
109.								
110. Floor Director								
111. Preproduction								
112. Production								
113. Postproduction								
114.								
115. Production Assistant								
116. Preproduction								
117. Production								
118. Postproduction								
119.								

PRODUCTION STAFF (Con't)

CREW	ESTIMATED				ACTUAL			
	Days	Rate	O/T Hrs	Total	Days	Rate	O/T Hrs	Total
120. Teleprompter Operator								
121. Preproduction								
122. Production								
123. Postproduction								
124.								
125. Telecine Operator								
126. Preproduction								
127. Production								
128. Postproduction								
129.								
130. Other Crew								
131.								
132. Miscellaneous								
133.								
134.								
	Subtotal							

CAMERA, VIDEOTAPE RECORDING, VIDEO ENGINEERING

DESCRIPTION	ESTIMATED				ACTUAL			
	Days	Rate	O/T Hrs	Total	Days	Rate	O/T Hrs	Total
135. Camera Operator No.( )								
136. Preproduction								
137. Production								
138. Postproduction								
139. VTR Operator								
140. Preproduction								
141. Production								
142. Postproduction								
143. Video Engineer								
144. Preproduction								
145. Production								
146. Postproduction								
147. Other Crew								
148. Preproduction								
149. Production								
150. Postproduction								
151.								
152. Equipment Rental								
153. Equipment Purchases								
154. Maintenance/Repair								
155.								
156. Miscellaneous								
157.								
	Subtotal							

SET DESIGN, CONSTRUCTION, DECORATION, AND PROPERTIES

DESCRIPTION	ESTIMATED				ACTUAL			
	Days	Rate	O/T Hrs	Total	Days	Rate	O/T Hrs	Total
158. Set Designer								
159. Artist								
160. Construction Labor								
161.								
162. Construction Materials								
163.								
164. Miscellaneous								
165.								
166. Set Decorator								
167. Preproduction								
168. Production								
169. Postproduction								
170. Set Dressing Labor								
171.								
172. Set Properties								
173. Set Dressing Props								
174. Cleaning/Loss/Damage								
175. Purchases								
176. Rentals								
177.								
178. Miscellaneous								
179.								
180. Property Master								
181.								
182. Property Labor								
183. Vehicle(s)								
184.								
185. Action Props Rentals								
186. Action Props Purchased								
187. Cleaning/Loss/Damage								
188. Food								
189. Miscellaneous								
190.								
191. Grip(s)								
192.								
193. Crane/Dolly Crew								
194.								
195. Rentals								
196. Other								
197.								
198. Miscellaneous								
199.								
	Subtotal							

SET LIGHTING

DESCRIPTION	ESTIMATED				ACTUAL			
	Days	Rate	O/T Hrs	Total	Days	Rate	O/T Hrs	Total
200. Lighting Director								
201. Preproduction								
202. Production								
203. Postproduction								
204.								
205. Follow Spot Operator								
206. Expendables								
207. (gels, etc.)								
208. Light Instruments								
209. 1 kw Spot No. ( )								
210. 2 kw Spot No. ( )								
211. kw Spot No. ( )								
212. 1 kw Scoop No. ( )								
213. 1 1/2 kw Scoop No. ( )								
214. 2 kw Scoop No. ( )								
215. kw Scoop No. ( )								
216. Ellipsoidal Spotlight								
217. Follow Spot								
218. Broad/Softlight No. ( )								
219. Strip/Cyc Light No. ( )								
220.								
221. Equipment Rentals								
222.								
223. Equipment Purchases								
224.								
225. Miscellaneous								
226.								
	Subtotal							

AUDIO PRODUCTION

DESCRIPTION	ESTIMATED				ACTUAL			
	Days	Rate	O/T Hrs	Total	Days	Rate	O/T Hrs	Total
227. Audio Director								
228. Preproduction								
229. Production								
230. Postproduction								
231. Mike Grip(s)								
232. Preproduction								
233. Production								
234. Postproduction								
235. Boom Operator(s)								
236. Preproduction								
237. Production								
238. Postproduction								

AUDIO PRODUCTION (Con't)

DESCRIPTION	ESTIMATED				ACTUAL			
	Days	Rate	O/T Hrs	Total	Days	Rate	O/T Hrs	Total
239. Microphones								
240. Lavaliere No. ( )								
241. Handheld No. ( )								
242. Boom No. ( )								
243. Wireless No. ( )								
244. Desk No. ( )								
245. Stand No. ( )								
246.								
247. Miscellaneous Labor								
248. Equipment Rentals								
249. Equipment Purchases								
250. Miscellaneous								
251.								
	Subtotal							

WARDROBE, MAKE-UP, AND HAIRSTYLING

DESCRIPTION	ESTIMATED				ACTUAL			
	Days	Rate	O/T Hrs	Total	Days	Rate	O/T Hrs	Total
252. Wardrobe Purchases								
253. Preproduction								
254. Production								
255. Postproduction								
256.								
257. Wardrobe Rentals								
258.								
259. Loss/Damage								
260. Dyeing/Cleaning								
261. Miscellaneous								
262.								
263. Hairstylist								
264.								
265. Make-up Supplies								
266.								
267. Hairstyling Supplies								
268. Miscellaneous								
269.								
	Subtotal							

VIDEOTAPE STOCK

DESCRIPTION	ESTIMATED				ACTUAL			
	Days	Rate	O/T Hrs	Total	Days	Rate	O/T Hrs	Total
270. Videotape:								
271. 1" (:) x ($)								
272. 3/4" (:20) x ($)								
273. 3/4" (:30) x ($)								
274. 3/4" (:60) x ($)								
275.								
276.								
	Subtotal							

POSTPRODUCTION EDITING

DESCRIPTION	ESTIMATED				ACTUAL			
	Days	Rate	O/T Hrs	Total	Days	Rate	O/T Hrs	Total
277. Technical Director								
278.								
279. Editing Suite Rental								
280. Master Tape Stock								
281. SMPTE Coding								
282. Sound Effects								
283. Dupes ( ) x ($)per								
284. Miscellaneous								
285.								
	Subtotal							

MUSIC

DESCRIPTION	ESTIMATED				ACTUAL			
	Days	Rate	O/T Hrs	Total	Days	Rate	O/T Hrs	Total
286. Music Purchases								
287. Music Royalties								
288. Recording Facility								
289.								
290. Audio Recording Tape								
291.								
292. Miscellaneous								
293.								
	Subtotal							

COMMENTS

PROGRAM FORMAT
MULTIPLE CAMERA VIDEO TALK SHOW/ENTERTAINMENT PROGRAM PRODUCTION

SEGMENT	CONTENTS	TIME	RUNNING/BACK TIME
OPENING	NOTES		00:00 / 28:30
			__:__ / __:__
Commercial Break		__:__	__:__ / __:__
UNIT ONE			
			__:__ / __:__
Commercial Break		__:__	__:__ / __:__
UNIT TWO			
			__:__ / __:__
Commercial Break		__:__	__:__ / __:__
UNIT THREE			
			__:__ / __:__
Commercial Break		__:__	__:__ / __:__
CLOSING			28:30 / 00:00

PROGRAM SET DESIGN
MULTIPLE CAMERA VIDEO TALK SHOW/ENTERTAINMENT PROGRAM PRODUCTION

Producer:

Date: / /

Program Title:

Set Title:

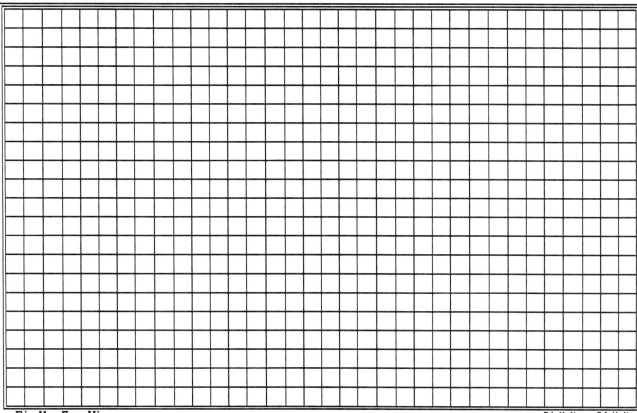

Bird's Eye View

21 Units x 34 Units

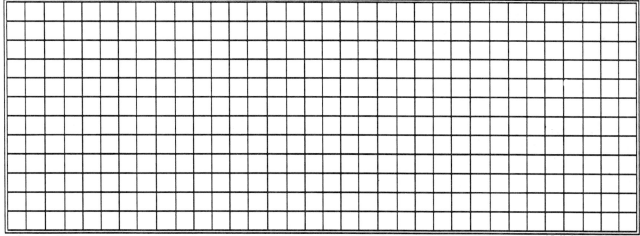

Front View

12 Units x 34 Units

STUDIO SET PROPERTIES LIST
MULTIPLE CAMERA VIDEO TALK SHOW/ENTERTAINMENT PROGRAM PRODUCTION

Producer: Program Title:

Date: /   /

Set Properties: includes furniture (desk, chairs, tables, etc.)   Acquired   Date

1.
2.
3.
4.
5.
6.
7.
8.
9.
10.

Set Decorations: includes hand props, set appointments (plants, books, telephone, etc.)   Acquired   Date

1.
2.
3.
4.
5.
6.
7.
8.
9.
10.

Notes:

TITLING/OPENING DESIGN
MULTIPLE CAMERA VIDEO TALK SHOW/ENTERTAINMENT PROGRAM PRODUCTION

Producer:

Program Title:

Date: /   /

Page   of

VIDEO	AUDIO

VIDEO	AUDIO

GRAPHIC DESIGN REQUEST
MULTIPLE CAMERA VIDEO TALK SHOW/ENTERTAINMENT PROGRAM PRODUCTION

Producer:

Graphic Artist:

Deadline: /   /

Program Title:

Date: /   /

Page   of

Graphic No. ☐

Image Design:

Text:

Graphic No. ☐

Image Design:

Text:

Graphic No. ☐

Image Design:

Text:

Graphic No. □

Image Design:

Text:

Graphic No. □

Image Design:

Text:

Graphic No. □

Image Design:

Text:

Graphic No. □

Image Design:

Text:

FACILITY REQUEST
MULTIPLE CAMERA VIDEO TALK SHOW/ENTERTAINMENT PROGRAM PRODUCTION

Production Facility: Day of Week: Hours: : to :

Producer: Program Title:
Director: Airing Frequency: □daily □weekly □_____
Date: / /   Starting Production Date: / /   Program Length: :

Facility Space: □_____
□Studio   □Audio Control Room   □Set Construction Workshop
□Control Room   □Make-Up Room   □Costume Storage
□Master Control   □Dressing Room   □Property Storage

Studio Requirements:
□No. Studio Cameras   □Teleprompter   □No. Floor Monitors
   Light Instruments   □_____   □Audio Boom Platform
   □__kw spots □__kw scoops □ellipsoidal spotlight □follow spot □broad/softlight
   □__kw spots □__kw scoops □strip/cyc lights □other_____

Control Room Requirements: □_____
□Production Switcher   □Character Generator   □Intercom Network: no. stations___
□DVE   □Still Store/E-men   □Light Control Board

Master Control Area Requirements:
□Videotape Decks   □Telecine   □_____
   □record machines   □35mm slides
   □playback machines   □16mm film

Audio Control Room Requirements:
□Audio Control Board   □Studio Foldback   □_____
□Playback Input Units:
   □audio cartridge □audio cassette □reel-to-reel □turntable □compact disc
□Microphones:
   □lavaliere □handheld □boom □wireless □desk □stand

Preproduction Requirements:
   Set Construction/Decoration: Date: / /   Hours: : to :
                                Date: / /   Hours: : to :
                                  Date: / /   Hours: : to :
   Set Lighting: Date: / /   Hours: : to :
                     Date: / /   Hours: : to :
                     Date: / /   Hours: : to :
   Program Rehearsals: Date: / /   Hours: : to :
                           Date: / /   Hours: : to :
                           Date: / /   Hours: : to :

Studio Production Personnel:

Production Role	Personnel	Facility Crew	Program Crew
Director		☐	☐
Assistant Director		☐	☐
_____		☐	☐
Production Assistant		☐	☐
_____		☐	☐
Technical Director		☐	☐
Lighting Director		☐	☐
_____		☐	☐
Audio Director		☐	☐
Microphone Boom Operator		☐	☐
Microphone Grip		☐	☐
_____		☐	☐
_____		☐	☐
Floor Director		☐	☐
_____		☐	☐
Teleprompter Operator		☐	☐
_____		☐	☐
Camera Operator 1		☐	☐
Camera Operator 2		☐	☐
Camera Operator 3		☐	☐
Camera Operator 4		☐	☐
_____		☐	☐
Telecine Operator		☐	☐
_____		☐	☐
Videotape Recorder Operator		☐	☐
_____		☐	☐
Video Engineer		☐	☐
_____		☐	☐
_____		☐	☐
_____		☐	☐

TALENT AUDITION
MULTIPLE CAMERA VIDEO TALK SHOW/ENTERTAINMENT PROGRAM PRODUCTION

Producer:	Program Title:

Host/Hostess/Moderator: Telephone:
Address: Home ( ) -
City: Work ( ) -
State: Zip Code: Birthdate: / /

Availability Unavailability
 Dates: Hours: Dates: Hours:

Personal Data: Height Weight Ethnicity:
 Hat Size: Shoe Size: Waist Measurement: Chest Measurement:
 In Seam: Shirt/Blouse Size: Suit/Dress Size:

Agent:
Union Affiliation:

Please explain your interest in this production:

Please list other experiences that you feel qualify you for the role of host/hostess/
 moderator for this talk show/entertainment program:

Make any additional comments about your qualifications for this role:

PLEASE ATTACH YOUR RESUME AND PHOTO TO THIS FORM, OR LIST PREVIOUS EXPERIENCE
AND/OR DRAMA TRAINING ON THE REVERSE SIDE OF THIS FORM.

GUEST BIOGRAPHICAL INFO

MULTIPLE CAMERA VIDEO TALK SHOW/ENTERTAINMENT PROGRAM PRODUCTION

Producer: Program Title:

Interviewer: Date: /   /

Guest Name:

Home Address:

City: State/Country: Zip:

Age: Weight: Height:

Marital Status: ☐ married   ☐ single   ☐ divorced   ☐ widow(er)

Spouse's Name:

Children: ☐ yes   ☐ no

   Names of Children:

Telephone: Home (   )   -   Work (   )   -

Present Occupation:

Employer:

Past Occupations of Interest:

Educational Background:

Hobbies of Interest/Talent:

List questions you might suggest the program host(ess) ask you.

1.

2.

3.

4.

5.

GUEST BOOKING
MULTIPLE CAMERA VIDEO TALK SHOW/ENTERTAINMENT PROGRAM PRODUCTION

Program Title: _____ Taping Date: / / Air Date: / /

Guest Name:
Home Address:
City: State/Country: Zip:
Telephone: Home: ( ) - Business: ( ) -

Program Category:
- ☐ Talk Program ☐
- ☐ Music ☐
- ☐ Other Entertainment ☐

Recommended by:

Purpose of Appearance:

Key Achievements:

On-Air Support Material(s):
- ☐ Film (16mm) ☐ 35mm Slides ☐
- ☐ Video ☐ Photographs ☐
  - ☐ 2" ☐ 3/4" ☐
  - ☐ 1" ☐ 1/2"

Booking Arrangements:
Reimbursement:
- ☐ Travel ☐ Mileage ☐ Other | Amount: $ |

Accommodations:
- ☐ Hotel ☐ program budget ☐ publicist ☐ agent
- ☐ Transportation ☐ hotel ☐ studio ☐ publicist ☐ agent | Amount: $ |

Notes:

Miscellaneous Information:

Confirmation:
Notification   Response
- ☐ Mail   Date: / /   ☐ Mail   Date: / /
- ☐ Telephone Date: / /   ☐ Telephone   Date: / /

CAMERA BLOCKING PLOT
MULTIPLE CAMERA VIDEO TALK SHOW/ENTERTAINMENT PROGRAM PRODUCTION

Director:

Date: / /

Set:

Program Title:

Page   of

Lighting
- ☐ _____
- ☐ _____
- ☐ _____
- ☐ _____

Sound
- ☐ _____
- ☐ _____
- ☐ _____

Bird's Eye Floor Plan

Cameras /Properties/Blocking

Description: Cameras/Movement/Properties

In-cue   Dialogue/Action   Out-cue   Dialogue/Action

Comments:

CAMERA SHOT LIST
MULTIPLE CAMERA VIDEO TALK SHOW/ENTERTAINMENT PROGRAM PRODUCTION

Camera Operator:
Camera: C1 C2 C3
Date: /   /

Program Title:
Studio Production Date: /   /
Set:

SHOT No.	CAMERA FRAMING	TALENT	CAMERA MOVEMENT	SPECIAL INSTRUCTIONS

SET LIGHTING PLOT
MULTIPLE CAMERA VIDEO TALK SHOW/ENTERTAINMENT PROGRAM PRODUCTION

Lighting Director:

Producer:

    Approval ☐

Set:

Program Title:

Date: /   /

Page   of

Lighting

☐ ———————
☐ ———————
☐ ———————

Lighting
   Change
☐ Yes
☐ No

Bird's Eye Floor Plan   Cameras/Properties/Blocking

Description: Cameras/Movement/Properties

Lighting Instruments
    Key Lights:

    Fill Lights:

    Soft Lights:

Lighting Accessories
    Barn Doors:

    Flags:

    Gobo:

Filters
    Spun Glass:

    Gels:

    Scrims:

Windows
    Daylight:

    Night time:

    Dusk:

    Change:

Property Lights
    Lamps:

    Ceiling:

    Other:

In-cue	Dialogue/Action Lighting Change Cue	Out-cue	Dialogue/Action Lighting Change Cue

AUDIO PLOT
MULTIPLE CAMERA VIDEO TALK SHOW/ENTERTAINMENT PROGRAM PRODUCTION

Audio Director:

Producer:

   Approval ☐

Date: /   /

Program Title:

Set:

Sound
☐ Synchronous
☐ Silent
☐ _____

Microphone
☐ Directional
☐ Wireless
☐ _____

Microphone Support
☐ Fishpole
☐ Giraffe
☐ Handheld
☐ Hanging
☐ _____

Sound Effects
☐ Foldback
☐ _____

Bird's Eye Floor Plan

Cameras/Properties/Blocking
Microphone Grip(s)/Microphone Support(s)/Cable Run(s)
Sound Perspective: ☐ close   ☐ distant

Description: Cameras/Movement/Properties

In-cue	Dialogue/Action	Out-cue	Dialogue/Action

Rights/Clearance Required:

SOUND EFFECTS/MUSIC PLOT
MULTIPLE CAMERA VIDEO TALK SHOW/ENTERTAINMENT PROGRAM PRODUCTION

Audio Director:	Program Title:
	Program Length: :
Producer:	Date: / /
Approval:	

Summary of Program Sound Effects/Music Needs

EFFECT	MUSIC	SOURCE	LENGTH	PROGRAM FORMAT CUES
				in-cue
			:	out-cue
				in-cue
			:	out-cue
				in-cue
			:	out-cue
				in-cue
			:	out-cue
				in-cue
			:	out-cue
				in-cue
			:	out-cue
				in-cue
			:	out-cue

Rights/Clearances

COPYRIGHTED MATERIAL	PUBLISHER	COPYRIGHT OWNER	CLEARANCE(S) NEEDED

Prerecorded Audio Tracks

CONTENT/COPY	WRITER/COMPOSER	NARRATOR/ARTIST	RECORDED
			/ /
			/ /
			/ /

CHARACTER GENERATOR COPY
MULTIPLE CAMERA VIDEO TALK SHOW/ENTERTAINMENT PROGRAM PRODUCTION

Producer:
Production Assistant:
Date: /   /

Program Title:
Production Date:
Page   of

SLATE

Title:
Producer:
Director:
Length: :
Taping Date: /   /
Air Date: /   /

Record No.

GUEST
LOWER
THIRD

Record No.

PROGRAM
TITLE

Record No.

Record No.

TALENT
LOWER
THIRD

Host

Record No.

■ File tape

VIDEO/FILM
CREDIT

Record No.

LOWER
THIRD

Record No.

■ Courtesy of

COURTESY
CREDIT

Record No.

Record No.

Record No.

Record No.

Record No.

Record No.

Record No.

Record No.

Record No.

CLOSING CREDITS

<u>Video Engineer</u>

<u>Videotape Recording</u>

<u>Lighting Director</u>

<u>Telecine</u>

Record No.

Record No.

<u>Studio Camera Operators</u>

<u>Studio Prompter Operator</u>

<u>Floor Director</u>

Record No.

Record No.

<u>Audio Director</u>

<u>Production Assistant</u>

<u>Assistant Director</u>

<u>Technical Director</u>

Record No.

Record No.

Director

Producer

Record No.

Copyright 1990

Record No.

FORMAT/RUNDOWN SHEET
MULTIPLE CAMERA VIDEO TALK SHOW/ENTERTAINMENT PROGRAM PRODUCTION

SEGMENT	CONTENTS	TIME	RUNNING/BACK TIME
OPENING	NOTES (Guests, Character Generator Copy, Unit Summary, etc.)		00:00 / 28:30
		__:__	
		__:__	
		__:__	
		__:__	
			__:__ / __:__
Commercial Break		__:__	__:__ / __:__
UNIT ONE			
		__:__	
		__:__	
		__:__	
		__:__	
		__:__	
		__:__	
		__:__	
		__:__	
			__:__ / __:__
Commercial Break		__:__	__:__ / __:__
UNIT TWO			
		__:__	
		__:__	
		__:__	
			__:__ / __:__
Commercial Break		__:__	__:__ / __:__
UNIT THREE			
		__:__	
		__:__	
			__:__ / __:__
Commercial Break		__:__	__:__ / __:__
CLOSING			
		__:__	
			28:30 / 00:00

DIRECTOR'S CHECKLIST
MULTIPLE CAMERA VIDEO TALK SHOW/ENTERTAINMENT PROGRAM PRODUCTION

Director: Program Title:
Taping Date:

Assistant Director:
☐ Ready   time   :   Problem(s)/Delay:

Technical Director:
☐ Ready   time   :   Problem(s)/Delay

Production Assistant:
☐ Ready   time   :   Problem(s)/Delay

Audio Director:
☐ Ready   time   :   Problem(s)/Delay

Floor Director:
☐ Ready   time   :   Problem(s)/Delay

Camera 1 Operator:
Camera 2 Operator:
Camera 3 Operator:
☐ Ready   time   :   Problem(s)/Delay

Videotape Recorder Operator:
☐ Ready   time   :   Problem(s)/Delay

Video Engineer:
☐ Ready   time   :   Problem(s)/Delay

Talent:
☐ Ready   time   :   Problem(s)/Delay

Telecine Operator:
☐ Ready   time   :   Problem(s)/Delay

Producer:
☐ Ready   time   :   Problem(s)/Delay

Production Meeting Notes:

Chapter 4

Description and Glossary for Studio Production Organizing Forms

INTRODUCTION

A barometer to successful television production is the degree to which producing and production tasks are accomplished and the extent to which producing and production tasks are *successfully* accomplished. Equally important to successful accomplishment of those tasks is the knowledge and awareness of the details necessary at each talk show/entertainment program producing and production task stage.

This chapter presents a description and glossary of terms for successful studio talk show/entertainment program production task accomplishment. These descriptions and glossaries are presented in terms of the organizing forms found in Chapter 3. Each organizing form is presented here by title, the particular production process to which it refers, the producing and/or production personnel responsible for the completion of the form and the tasks, and a description of the purpose of the form and of the objective in using the form.

Not all of the organizing forms are necessary or even required in every studio talk show/entertainment program production. They are selective and designed to be used as needed. Those forms that organize and assist in accomplishing a studio talk show/entertainment program producing, production, or postproduction task should be tried for the ease and thoroughness with which it organizes a task. Those forms that are redundant to a particular program production should be ignored. The forms are meant to be a help, not a stumbling block, to studio talk show/entertainment program production.

• Program Proposal Form

Production process Talk show/entertainment program preproduction

Responsibility Producer

Purpose To propose to management personnel at a television station, cable system, or public service organization the proposed design and production of a new television program.

Objective The program proposal form organizes all essential elements necessary to suggest and design a new television program for interested parties. The proposal spells out (1) program title and the rationale for it, (2) program length with commercial breaks, (3) preproduction and production time required, (4) suggested airing time, (5) the format description of the program, and (6) proposed sponsorship.

The program proposal serves as a cover form to other preproduction documents in the development of a new television program. Additional documentation that should be included with the program proposal is at least the program treatment, program budget, and preproduction script. Other documentation might include a set design and a program format.

Glossary

Producer The name of the producer developing the concept and idea for the new program is entered here.

Date The date of proposal development goes here.

Page of This enumeration alerts a reader to the expected number of pages included in the proposal and to the number of the individual page.

Proposed Program Title The title of the proposed program is written here. Titles are very important. Titles for television programs should be short and be chosen to capture the essence of the program.

Rationale Administrative personnel judging the merits of a proposed program title will require some explanation for the title choice. That rationale should be entered here.

Proposed Program Length The length in minutes and seconds of the proposed program is entered here. The entry should be in terms of total time from first audio or video to closing audio or video. This time should include the time for commercial breaks (e.g., 28:30 for a half-hour program).

Proposed Number of Breaks/Commercials The number of proposed breaks will allow the calculation of real program length together with the length of the breaks.

Break Length The length of a break is entered here. This time multiplied by the total number of breaks and subtracted from the program length time will give the actual length of the program.

Proposed Network/Station/Production Facility The name of the television network, station, or production facility at which the proposed program would be produced is entered here. This is the name of the television production facility at which the proposed program is being produced (but not necessarily broadcast or cablecast).

Production Requirements The elements of production that will be required in the production of the proposed program should be listed here. This includes such elements as studio, control room, master control, telecine, digital video effects (DVE), character generator.

Production Crew Requirements The television production crew personnel required to produce the proposed program are listed here. Crew must be listed by role requirements (e.g., director, technical director, telecine operator).

Studio Production Hours The total number of weekly studio production hours required to produce the program is entered here. Four times the length of the program time is a rule of thumb for estimating studio production time (e.g., a half-hour program should take a two-hour block of studio production time).

Postproduction Hours The estimation of the time that may be required in postproduction, if necessary, should be entered here.

Proposed Telecast Time: Day/Time The time that the producer proposes as an ideal broadcast (or cablecast) time by day of the week and time of the day should be entered here.

Alternate Time(s): Day/Time Alternate days and times for the suggested telecast should be entered here.

Style/Format of the Proposed Program The producer describes the style or format of the proposed program here. The style or format is the particular genre of television program in which the proposed program fits. For example, the talk show genre is a style of program and suggests the format or order of the program; an amateur talent program indicates a style and suggests a format for the program.

Proposed/Suggested Sponsorship The producer suggests who or what product(s) might consider sponsoring the proposed program.

Attached The producer should check the appropriate box(es) of additional documents that will be included with the program proposal form.

- **Program Treatment Form**

Production process Talk show/entertainment program preproduction

Responsibility Producer

Purpose To verbally describe a new television program concept to a television station, cable system operator, or public service organization.

Objective The program treatment form attempts to verbally focus elements of the proposed program for the producer as a step toward presenting the idea or concept to a television station, cable system operator, or public service organization for approval.

The basic requirements of the production management or sponsors on which the appropriateness of a program will be judged include (1) the goals and objectives for the program, (2) a list of the demographics of the target audience, (3) some verbal description of the proposed program, (4) the choice of production values to relate to the demographics of the target audience, and (5) a production statement capturing the concept of the production.

For a program proposal, the treatment is the first of at least three basic documents—treatment, budget, and preproduction script—that comprise a proposal to management personnel or potential sponsors.

Glossary

Producer The name of the producer who is writing the proposal treatment is entered here.

Proposed Title A working title is appropriate to the proposed program described in the treatment. There is an advantage to titling a proposed program: A simple title can contain a concept or idea that paragraphs cannot convey.

Program Length The program length commitment gives management personnel and potential sponsors a grasp of the likelihood of the success of the program and its content in terms of its length.

Date This is the date of the creation of the treatment.

Page of This entry alerts a reader to the total number of pages to expect from the treatment and to the number of each individual page.

Program Goals and Objectives A statement of the goals and objectives for the proposed program should include the rationale for doing the proposed program as well as a description of the target audience, the audience's need for the program in terms of the topic, and the audience's interest in the topic. The more information that can be given in this section of the treatment form aids the management personnel or sponsors in judging the suitability of the proposed program.

Target Audience The target audience for the proposed program should be described here. In addition to giving a range of ages for the target audience, other qualities should be listed and described. Any demographic of the target audience will assist in choosing production values to hook the target audience.

Program Description   The program description is the verbal description of the proposed program, including proposed guests, guidelines for the guests, and possible themes for future programs. The more information that is available at this stage of preproduction the better management personnel or sponsors can judge the treatment for approval.

Production Values   The producer should choose those production values that relate to the demographics of the target audience. A production value is any television video or audio element or technique that is part of television production. An example of a production value related to an audience demographic is the choice of theme music appropriate to the age group of the target audience.

Production Statement   A production statement is a very brief emotional or rational verbal expression, which will function as a reminder throughout the program's production, of the specific goal or objective of the program. The production statement is meant to be a constant reminder to crew members of the precise goal of the production.

● **Preproduction Script Form**

Production process   Talk show/entertainment program preproduction

Responsibility   Producer

Purpose   To help the producer describe the proposed program by verbally and visually suggesting what a general program script might look like.

Objective   The preproduction is a recommended document as part of a new television program proposal. The preproduction script is a preliminary draft of a script. It provides the producer with a description in video and audio columns of the look and sound of a generalized unit of the proposed program's series. The preproduction script would be important for suggesting opening and closing copy and the order of the proposed program.

Glossary

Producer   The name of the producer who is designing and developing the proposal for the new television program is entered here.

Program Title   The title for the proposed program is entered here.

Date   The date of the development of the preproduction script is indicated here.

Page of   The total number of pages of the preproduction script and each individual page number are entered here.

Video   The proposed video images of the new program are described in this column. The producer should indicate both the content of the images and the framing of the screen image for every change in the sequence of images proposed. Title and character generator copy should be indicated in this column. For example,

VIDEO

XLS New York City skyline;
Diss to MS tenement;
Cut to CU Michael Woods

Super LT   MICHAEL WOODS
          Producer

Audio   The proposed audio copy for the new program is written in this column. The copy should indicate who is to speak the copy and what the announcer is to say. The audio copy should be typed in capital letters. For example,

AUDIO

SFX: City street traffic sounds
ANN: NOT EVERYONE LIVING IN
NEW YORK CITY SUFFERS FROM
THE IMPERSONALIZATION OF THE
BIG APPLE.

● **Production Budget Form**

Production process   Talk show/entertainment program preproduction

Responsibility   Producer

Purpose   To realistically estimate all possible costs of the production of the proposed program from preproduction to postproduction.

Objective   The budget form is a model of a budget for the production of a talk show/entertainment program. The form will help to estimate as many expenses of multiple camera talk show/entertainment program production as possible and, after production, to help translate them into actual expenses. It serves to suggest possible cost items across the spectrum of studio video production, personnel, equipment, labor, time, and materials. The form should be used to suggest expenses and to call attention to possible hidden costs before production begins.

General comments on the use of the budget form   The budget form should be studied for line items that might pertain to a proposed multiple camera talk show/entertainment program production. Only applicable line items for the proposed program need to be considered. Use the suggestion of line items to weight as many foreseeable costs as possible for the project.

Note that all sections of the budget are summarized on the front page of the form. The subtotal from each section is brought forward to be listed in this summary.

Some costs are calculated by the number of days employed, the hourly rate of pay, and overtime hours. Other costs are calculated by the number of items or people divided by the allotted amount of money per day for the item or person. The cost of materials is calculated by the amount of material(s) multiplied by the cost of a unit.

Most cost entry columns of this budget form are labeled "Days, Rate, O/T [overtime] Hrs, Total." For those line items that do not involve day and rate, the total column alone should be used.

The number of produced programs accounted for is important to a budget of this sort. This number represents the number of programs in a proposed series or television season. Budget line figures will be a multiple of the proposed number of programs in the series.

Projected costs to be applied to the budget can be determined from a number of sources. The rate card of a local video production facility is one source of equipment rental and production costs. Salary estimates and talent fees can be estimated from the going rates of relevant services of equivalent professionals or from their agencies. Cost quotes can be requested by telephone from providers of services and materials. Travel costs (for guests) can be obtained by phone calls to travel agencies or airline companies. Preparing a good budget involves a lot of time and research.

Glossary

Producer The name of the producer for the proposed program is entered here.

Director The name of the director of the proposed program is recorded in this entry. If a director has not yet been chosen or hired, the space can be left blank.

Date This is the date of the preparation of the program production budget.

Program Title The title for the proposed program should be entered here.

Length The length of the proposed program should be recorded here.

No. Preproduction Days Estimate the number of days to complete the necessary preproduction stages, including rehearsals. This estimate includes quality time on all preproduction stages (budget, set design, auditions, camera blocking, shot list, and rehearsal(s)) for all production crew members involved in the preproduction of the program (producer, director, camera operators, lighting director, videotape recorder operator, audio director, and talent).

No. Studio Production Days/Hours Estimate the number of days and hours for which the studio or control room facilities may be needed in the production of the program. This time estimate accounts for all in-studio videotaping (e.g., talent on a set) and the use of the control room switcher or character generator for postproduction effects.

No. Postproduction Days/Hours Estimate the number of days and hours that will be spent in postproduction in completing the program master edit.

First Production Date Indicate the date proposed to begin studio production and videotaping of the program.

No. Programs in Series The proposed budget has to account for the number of programs covered by the budget. This entry records the number of proposed programs in the series. For example, 52 programs would account for a weekly program for a year; 26 for a full season of programs, allowing for reruns during the off season; and 13 would comprise a half season.

Cost estimates throughout the budget will have to be multiplied by the number of programs in the series to estimate the particular line item costs for the series.

Summary of Production Costs This summary area brings forward the subtotals of the costs from each section within the budget form. Note that each line item in the summary section is found as a section head within the budget form. When the individual sections are completed, the subtotal is brought forward and listed in the summary section.

Contingency This term refers to the practice of adding a percentage of the subtotal to the subtotal as a pad against the difference between the estimated and the actual cost of all line items. The customary contingency is 15%. For example, multiply the subtotal in line 16 by 0.15 to determine the contingency figure. That result added to line 17 becomes the grand total of the program production budget.

Estimated The estimated costs refer to costs that can only be projected before the production. Rarely do the estimated costs match the final costs because of the number of variables that cannot be anticipated. Every attempt should be made to gather accurate estimated costs and to ensure the consideration of as many variables to the cost as possible. The challenge of estimating costs is to project as closely as possible to the actual costs.

Actual The actual costs are the costs that are incurred for the respective line items during or after production is completed. The actual costs are those costs that will really be paid for the production. The ideal budget attempts to have actual costs be as close as possible— either at or, preferably, under—to the estimated costs for the production.

Rights and Clearances This section lists the costs that might be incurred in obtaining necessary clearances for copyrighted program elements, music synchronization rights, and royalty payment.

Producer and Staff Expenses This section of the budget accounts for the producer of the program and other personnel who may have producing responsibilities. For purposes of estimating cost, the role of the producer is divided into the three areas of a video production: preproduction, production, and postproduction.

Director and Staff Expenses This section covers the director and personnel associated with the directing responsibilities. As with most budgets, some line items, such as personnel (e.g., secretary), are listed for purposes of suggesting enlarged staffs and additional roles during program production. They are not necessary to all studio talk show/entertainment program productions.

Talent The expenses incurred by the talent associated with the production of the program are accounted for in this section. Some talent may be hired by contract and may be subject to other fees (e.g., Screen Actors Guild (SAG)). Other talent may be freelancers. Provision must be made in the budget for guest(s) on the program; their travel and accommodations must be included in the budget.

Benefits Depending on the arrangements made with talent, some production budgets may have to account for benefits accruing to talent and crew (e.g., health insurance and pensions). Insurance coverage and state and federal taxes that are due to salaries paid to talent and crew members should be accounted for in this section.

Production Facility   This section lists production facility space required for the production of the program. For each facility space, the rate for the technical hardware that may be needed should be included. Rate cards for production facilities will offer breakdown lists for these spaces and the technical hardware in them. The producer will have to choose what is needed and the projected cost of each.

Production Staff   This section accounts for production staff and crew members for each stage of the production of the program—preproduction, production, and postproduction.

Cameras, Videotape Recording, and Video Engineering   Those personnel and expenses that function with the maintenance and use of the studio cameras are accounted for in this section. The equipment that may need to be purchased or rented should be recorded here. Camera equipment rental will be necessary if any exterior stock shots have to be taken for the program.

Set Design, Construction, Decoration, Properties   Program production will involve the use of studio sets (even the cyclorama is considered a set). Budget consideration is made for set design, construction, and decoration. This section of the budget suggests some set design and construction personnel and some set construction materials and decoration costs.

Most program sets require properties, action properties (e.g., vehicles or animals), or hand properties (e.g., a telephone). This section of the budget suggests and accounts for personnel, action and hand properties, and the care and handling of the properties for the production.

Set Lighting   The requirement to create a mood and a setting on studio sets accounts for the personnel and equipment for set lighting. Studio costs can be incurred with the use of light instruments. The budget form requires the listing of individual light instruments necessary to light the studio set for production.

Audio Production   Audio production and recording are essential to program production. This section of the budget suggests personnel, hardware (e.g., microphones), and equipment rental and purchase line items for the production.

Wardrobe, Make-up and Hairstyling   Talent requires wardrobe consideration. Wardrobe personnel, acquisition, and care are accounted for in this section.

Make-up and hair preparation are also necessary for the talent. This section of the budget suggests some line items to be accounted for when make-up, hairstyling, and supplies are required.

Videotape Stock   The provision of necessary videotape stock in the required sizes is accounted for in this section.

Postproduction Editing   The personnel, facilities, and materials for postproduction during editing are accounted for in this section of the budget.

Music   Because most talk show/entertainment program production will involve music, original or recorded, this section of the budget lists some of the potential costs and personnel involved in obtaining or recording the music.

- **Program Format Form**

Production process   Talk show/entertainment program preproduction

Responsibility   Producer

Purpose   To design, describe, and define the elements of the proposed program and the order of presentation of those elements.

Objective   The program format provides the design of the proposed program. It contains the units of the program and the breaks that separate the units. The format also indicates the order of the units and elements of the program.

Glossary

Segment   The segment defines the separate program units divided by commercial breaks that make up the program format.

Contents   This area defines those differing elements that will make up the program, such as a list of the guests.

Time   This area provides the cumulative time of the program. These entries will sum up the time for each of the elements in each program unit, including the time for the breaks, which will add up to the length of the program.

Running Time   This is the continuous time of the program beginning with zero.

Back Time   This is the continuous time of the program beginning with the length of the program (e.g., 28:30) and subtracting elements of the program to zero (the end of the program).

Opening   This area defines the first unit of the proposed program. The other sequential units, one, two, three, and closing, make up a model set of units for a program.

Notes   This area of the form describes those elements that make up the content of the unit.

Commercial Break   These breaks comprise the proposed opportunities within the program for commercials or public service announcements.

- **Program Set Design Form**

Production process   Talk show/entertainment program preproduction

Responsibility   Producer

Purpose   To design the studio set for the program.

Objective   The program set design form allows for the design of both a bird's eye view of a proposed program studio set and a front view. A 21 × 34 unit grid for a bird's eye view allows the assignment of any number of footage per unit to create a program set. The front view allows a 12 × 34 unit grid for the design.

Glossary

Producer The producer's name indicates either that the producer has designed the studio set for the proposed program or that the producer has played a consulting role in the approval of the set design.

Program Title The title for the proposed program is entered here.

Bird's Eye View The bird's eye view grid is an area for the proposed program set sketch or design from the top looking down. The 21 × 34 units allow the assignment of some uniform unit of measure to each unit of the grid (e.g., 1 square = 1 foot creates a 34-foot-wide set design area, 1 square = 2 feet creates a 68-foot-wide set design area). Breadth and depth of a proposed program set should be indicated on the grid.

Front View The front view grid is an area for the proposed program set sketch or design from the front looking straight toward the set. The 12 × 34 unit grid allows the assignment of some uniform measure to each unit of the grid (e.g., 1 square = 1 foot creates a 12-foot-high set design area, 1 square = 2 feet creates a 24-foot-high set design area).

- **Studio Set Properties List Form**

Production process Talk show/entertainment program preproduction

Responsibility Producer

Purpose To list the necessary studio set properties and decorations to be acquired for the completion of the set design.

Objective The studio set properties list catalogs the set properties required to complete the studio set design as approved by the producer. Two types of properties may be required: the set properties (e.g., chairs, desk, or coffee table), and set decorations (e.g., plants, statues, or telephone).

Glossary

Producer The name of the producer of the program is entered here.

Program Title The title of the program is entered here.

Date The date of the development of the list of the required properties is entered here.

Set Properties This list should contain those properties that are major set pieces, such as couch, chairs, coffee table, end tables, or desk. These pieces help define the set environment.

Acquired/Date When required properties are acquired, the date of acquisition should be indicated.

Set Decorations This list contains those properties that are often referred to as hand props; they include such items as plants, statuary, telephone, books for a bookcase, or ashtrays.

Acquired/Date When required properties are acquired, the date of acquisition should be indicated.

Notes The producer should indicate here any information about the above lists that will affect their purchase, acquisition, or use.

- **Titling/Opening Design Form**

Production process Talk show/entertainment preproduction

Responsibility Producer

Purpose To coordinate a verbal description of the titling and visual opening for the proposed program, as well as the proposed audio copy with corresponding storyboard frames.

Objective The video script and storyboard form is an alternative television script form in which each corresponding storyboard frame is coordinated with the verbal visual description and audio copy. Imaging the title and opening for the proposed program assists the producer in conveying the concept of the program to those who must judge its creativity and merit.

Glossary

Producer The name of the producer proposing the program is entered here.

Program Title The title of the proposed television program is entered here.

Date The date of the design of the title and opening is entered here.

Page of The total number of expected pages for the titling/opening design form is indicated here as is each individual page number.

Video This column is used in the same way as was the video column in the two column preproduction script form. It should contain a simplified verbal description of the video content, camera framing, edit transition, and character generator copy of the proposed video titling and opening sequences for the program.

Storyboard Frames Those storyboard frames that coordinate with the entry in the video column should be used. Not all frames will be needed or used. Simply skip those frames that do not match video and audio entries.

Audio This column is used in the same way as was the audio column in the two column preproduction script form. It will contain all audio copy for the proposed video sequences from the video column. The producer includes proposed theme music or sound effects that will accompany the visual images of the title and opening for the proposed program.

As with any television script, audio copy should be written and then the corresponding video descriptions should be created. On this form, the storyboard frame should be sketched corresponding to the first line of each new video column entry.

- **Graphic Design Request Form**

Production process Talk show/entertainment program preproduction

Responsibility Producer

Purpose To design those graphics needed as a matte or full screen video source during program production.

Objective This form allows the producer to request graphics for each program. Graphics or graphic design may be required for the title, for soliciting mail requests from viewers, or for providing a telephone number.

Glossary

Producer The name of the producer proposing the program is entered here.

Graphic Artist The name of the graphic artist responsible for the creation of the graphics is entered here.

Program Title The title of the proposed television program is entered here.

Date The date of the design of the title and opening is entered here.

Page of The total number of expected pages for the titling/opening design form is indicated here as is each individual page number.

Deadline Date The producer sets a deadline for the completion of the requested graphics. It is conceivable that some graphics could be for a future program and not just the current one.

Graphic No. The graphics being requested can be numbered consecutively for purposes of calculating the total number or for presenting the order in which each graphic is to be inserted into the program and should be indicated in this column.

Image Design This area permits the producer the opportunity to describe the content of a graphic's image or provide a verbal description of a graphic to be created.

Text This area of the form permits the producer to indicate any text required on the graphic. The text should be typed in this area in the exact form in which it should appear on the graphic.

- **Facility Request Form**

Production process Talk show/entertainment program preproduction

Responsibility Producer

Purpose To organize and request television production space and technical hardware from a video production facility for the program production.

Objective The facility request form allows the producer to choose from available television production facility space and television production hardware as a step in the program's production. This form prompts the producer to consider facility space and equipment, preproduction requirements, and production crew personnel.

Glossary

Production Facility The name of the production facility to which the facility request form will be submitted is entered here.

Day/Hours This information is the producer's choice for program production day of the week and hours within that day for studio videotaping.

Producer The name of the producer of the program is noted here.

Director The name of the director of the program is entered here.

Date The date on which the production facility request form was created is logged here.

Starting Production Date This entry indicates the first anticipated studio production date for this facility.

Program Title The title of the program is entered here.

Airing Frequency This information assists facility management in gauging the frequency of production studio use.

Program Length The telecast length of the program is indicated here.

Facility Space The producer chooses from among the possible facility spaces those that are required for the production of the program.

Studio Requirements The producer checks off those elements of the production studio hardware that will be required in the production of the program. In choosing the light instruments needed, the producer should indicate the number of each instrument needed and the kilowatts required.

Control Room Requirements The producer chooses the equipment in the control room that will be needed for the program production.

Master Control Area Requirements The equipment needed from the master control area for the production of the program is checked here. If more than one unit is required, the number of units should be entered instead of a check mark.

Audio Control Room Requirements The producer must place a check mark beside that equipment that will be required for the program. If more than one unit is required, the number of units should be entered in the box instead of a check mark.

Preproduction Requirements The producer must indicate to the production facility what preproduction time will be required for the production of the program. Preproduction requirements include set construction, set lighting, and rehearsal time.

Studio Production Personnel The producer must inquire of the production facility management what production crew personnel will be supplied by the facility and what personnel will have to be supplied by the producer. This area of the form permits listing the names of the crew members, and noting from which source they are coming.

- **Talent Audition Form**

Production process Talk show/entertainment program preproduction

Responsibility Producer

Purpose To gather and record relevant information at the time of talent auditions on the background and professional experience of prospective hosts, hostesses, or moderators for the program.

Objective The talent audition form is filled out by the prospective talent wishing to audition for the role of host, hostess, or moderator for the new program. Pertinent information is collected on this form that, along with an audition videotape, will allow the producer to make an enlightened choice for talent.

Glossary

Producer The name of the producer for the new program is entered here.

Program Title The title of the program is recorded here.

Host/Hostess/Moderator This area of personal demographic information is standard background data for each applicant.

Availability This area of the form screens for prospective talent availability to work program rehearsal(s) and videotaping sessions. Previous commitments may have to be altered based on this information.

Personal Data This area of the form gathers data that go on file for the program producer as data that may be relevant when wardrobe trades, for example, become available to the talent.

Agent It is important for the producer to know to what union or professional guilds a prospective talent belongs. This information may be necessary when payment of fees to these organizations come due.

Questions These three questions give the producer some open ended information from prospective talent on interest in the program, experience, and qualifications.

• **Guest Biographical Information Form**

Production process Talk show/entertainment program preproduction

Responsibility Producer

Purpose To collect relevant information on prospective guests on the program to be able to judge the suitability of the individual's appearance on the program.

Objective The guest biographical information form prompts prospective guests to provide the background information that a producer needs to decide whether the individual would make a suitable guest for the program.

Glossary

Producer The name of the producer proposing the program is entered here.

Program Title The title of the proposed television program is entered here.

Date The date that the form was completed is entered here.

Interviewer In the case where the guest does not complete the form but a member of the program's staff, an interviewer, does, the name of the interviewer goes here.

Guest Name The name of the individual to be considered as a guest for the program is entered here.

Home Address/City/State/Country/Zip This information is standard address information.

Age/Weight/Height This is standard personal identifying information.

Marital Status The marital status of the prospective guest is requested.

Spouse's Name If the prospective guest is married, the name of the spouse is entered here.

Children/Names of Children If the prospective guest has children, their names are entered here.

Telephone: Home/Work Both home and business telephone numbers of the prospective guest are entered here.

Present Occupation/Employer The occupation of the prospective guest and the employer are entered here.

Past Occupations of Interest The experience of previous occupations may be of interest to the program producer. That information is entered here.

Educational Background The educational history of the prospective guest is listed here.

Hobbies of Interest/Talent The special interests of the prospective guest are recorded here. For an entertainment program, the particular talent a prospective guest has is of special interest to the producer in deciding suitability for program appearance.

List of questions you might suggest the program host(ess) ask you This list prompts the prospective guest to provide the particular questions the individual would like to be asked and should focus on the reason for the guest's program appearance. It should be noted that the questions will not necessarily be asked, but that the prospective guest should prepare answers to the questions in the event of appearing on the program.

• **Guest Booking Form**

Production process Talk show/entertainment program preproduction

Responsibility Producer

Purpose To organize the appearance of guests on the program.

Objective The guest booking form organizes each guest's appearance on specific programs. This organizing information includes the program category for which a guest will appear, assigns the specific program and airing date, lists on-air support information, labels reimbursement amount, and describes accommodations and travel arrangements. The form also indicates notification of and confirmation from the guest on a program appearance.

Glossary

Program Title The title of the program being produced is recorded here.

Taping Date This is the date the individual program unit is being videotaped. If the program will be telecast live, the taping date is the same as the air date.

Air Date This is the date the particular program unit is being broadcast or cablecast.

Guest Name and Address This is general, standard guest background and contact information.

Program Category This area of the form indicates the type of program unit or program theme for which a guest might be suited.

Recommended by This records the name of the individual on the producing staff who makes the final recommendation for the specific guest's appearance on a program unit.

Purpose of Appearance   The recommending producer indicates why the particular guest should appear on the program.

Key Achievements   This category further specifies the reason why the particular guest should appear on a program unit.

On-Air Support Material(s)   Guests may have on-air support materials (e.g., books or videotapes) to augment their appearance on a program. The particular type of support materials should be noted.

Booking Arrangements/Reimbursement/Accommodations   This area of the form indicates the particular type of reimbursement and accommodations needed by a guest.

Reimbursement may be required for travel (e.g., air), mileage (e.g., for use of a private automobile), and any other of the guest's demands. The amount committed is listed in the "amount" box.

Accommodations indicate local housing and per diem that a guest may require while appearing on a program. Hotel and ground transportation resources are to be indicated, as well as the sources for funding those items. The amount committed is listed in the "amount" box.

Miscellaneous Information   The producer indicates any further information about guest booking that should be recorded for accounting purposes.

Confirmation   It is important to the producing staff that a guest's appearance be confirmed by the guest. This area of the form records the producer's notification of the appearance and the guest's confirmation of that appearance.

• Camera Blocking Plot Form

Production process   Talk show/entertainment program preproduction

Responsibility   Director

Purpose   To create the program format production design for the studio cameras from which the director will list camera shots, the lighting director will design the lighting plot, and the audio director will design the audio plot for the program.

Objective   The camera blocking plot prepares the director for all details for directing the program. From the approved set design and properties list the director can design all production elements for studio production videotaping.

The blocking plot records the blocking of talent and guest(s), cameras, and set proposed for production.

Some notes on the creation of the studio camera blocking plot form   The director should sketch the bird's eye view of the set from the set design form and properties list. The director should then position the talent and guest(s) in the floor plan and indicate the blocking placement and movement for the talent and guest(s). Then the studio cameras should be sketched into place to achieve the shot(s) as proposed in the preproduction

script and the titling/opening design form and program format/rundown sheet.

Glossary

Director   The program director's name is entered here.

Date   The date when the camera blocking plot is done is noted here.

Set   The name or label of the set for the program being blocked is entered here.

Program Title   The program title is written here.

Page of   The total number of pages of camera blocking plot forms is entered here together with each individual page number.

Lighting   The general lighting needs for the set are recorded in this column (e.g., special logo lighting or a chromakey panel).

Sound   The general sound pickup requirement is recorded here.

Bird's Eye Floor Plan   This is the area in which the bird's eye view of the set is sketched from the set design form for blocking purposes.

Cameras/Properties/Blocking   These are the elements to be entered on the bird's eye view of the set. Camera placement, set properties (e.g., furniture), and the placement and movement blocking of talent and guest(s) must be included.

Description   Any verbal description of the action of the program is recorded here. Some blocking may be better described in words than can be shown with the sketched blocking.

Cameras/Movement/Properties   These are the elements of the blocked set that are to be included in any description of the program unit being blocked.

In-cue/Dialogue/Action   The in-cue is the dialogue or action prompt that begins some element of the program.

Out-cue/Dialogue/Action   The out-cue is the dialogue or action prompt on which some program element ends.

Comments   This section allows the director to make additional notes on the blocking plot for the program. All thoughts should be jotted down during preproduction lest they be glossed over or forgotten during production meetings.

• Camera Shot List Form

Production process   Talk show/entertainment program preproduction

Responsibility   Director

Purpose   To translate the proposed camera blocking into a studio camera shot list for each camera.

Objective   The shot list form organizes the proposed studio camera blocking on the camera blocking plot into shots listed by studio camera. Each shot should generate the necessary video to create the proposed edits as designed on the preproduction script and format/rundown sheet. The shot list form will translate each proposed shot from preproduction script and the program format/rundown sheet to simpler lists for the advantage of the studio camera operators.

- **Glossary**

Camera Operator The name of the camera operator (each of the three) will be entered on this line.
Camera: C1, C2, C3 The camera assigned to each camera operator is indicated here by circling the appropriate camera number.
Program Title The title of the program is listed here.
Studio Production Date The date of the production session scheduled for the listed camera shots is entered here.
Set The set being used for the listed camera shots is recorded here.
Shot No. Every proposed shot needed to create the generalized camera shots for the program should be numbered consecutively on the shot list. The shot numbers are camera specific. The director separates the numbered shots and lists them for each camera in consecutive order. Each camera shot list will contain the numbered shot assigned to each camera. Those numbers are listed in this column.
Camera Framing Camera framing directions for each proposed shot should use the symbols for the basic camera shot framing: XLS, LS, MS, CU, or XCU. This will communicate to the camera operator the lens framing for the proposed shot.
Talent The content of each framed shot is indicated here. The director indicates who or what is framed in each shot. The object of framing can be the program talent, the guest(s), all persons on the set, or a logo.
Camera Movement Camera movement directions indicate the kind of camera movement designed for achieving the proposed shot. Camera movement in a shot may be primary movement, which is movement on the part of the talent in front of the camera. Primary movement will require camera movement—pan, tilt, or pedestal—to follow the talent or guest(s). This camera movement could be secondary movement, which is the movement of the camera itself. This camera movement could also be a dolly, truck or pedestal, or zoom. The director should translate those directions to this column for the camera operators.
Special Instructions The director may indicate some special instructions for a particular shot or camera operator. Those instructions should be indicated here. The camera shot list is camera specific, so an individual camera operator can be addressed in these special instructions.

- **Set Lighting Plot Form**

Production process Talk show/entertainment program preproduction

Responsibility Lighting director

Purpose To create and organize the lighting design of the program studio set.

Objective The lighting plot form is designed to facilitate the creation of the lighting design for the lighting director for the program set. The plot serves to preplan the placement of lighting instruments, kind of lighting, light-

ing control, and lighting design. When lighting is pre-planned, lighting equipment needs are easily realized and provided.

Notes on the use of the studio set lighting plot form
The lighting plot form encourages preplanning for lighting design and production. Hence, the more lighting needs and aesthetics that can be anticipated, the better the lighting production tasks. At a minimum, the studio set lighting design should be created in advance of re-hearsal(s). Lighting design can begin after the set construction is complete. The essentials basic to planning lighting design are the bird's eye floor plan and the talent and guest(s) blocking area of the set. This information is available from the producer's program format/rundown sheets, set design, and the director's camera blocking plot.

Glossary

Lighting Director The name of the lighting director for the production is entered here.
Producer Approval The lighting plot will have to be approved by the producer. The producer signs or initials approval on this form. Approval by the producer authorizes expenses in lighting needs acquisition for the production.
Set The lighting director indicates the name or label for the set being lighted.
Program Title The program's title is recorded here.
Date The date of the design of the studio set lighting plot is entered here.
Page of The total number of expected pages for the studio set lighting plot form is indicated here as is each individual page number.
Lighting This area of the plot notes any basic needs in lighting design (e.g., special logo lighting or chromakey area).
Light Change: Yes/No It is important to lighting design and lighting control to know if the program format indicates or the director plans any change of lighting during videotaping. This notation alerts the lighting director to that need.
Bird's Eye Floor Plan The best preproduction information for the lighting director is the floor plan for the set with talent and guest(s) blocking and movement area noted and camera placement indicated. This should be sketched in this box from the director's camera blocking form. Where the cameras are to be placed is important to the lighting director and lighting design.
Description Any director's notes on the elements of the program's production that will affect lighting design should be noted here.
Lighting Instruments/Lighting Accessories/Filters/Property Lights/Windows These lists in the lighting plot form are designed to assist the lighting director in considering all elements of lighting design and materials or situations in the preparation of the lighting plot. A lighting director can make notations in the proper space in planning for the particular design of each set.
In-cue A lighting director makes note of any in-cue from the program format form when—on what visual imaging or audio cue—the lighting design is to begin.

Out-cue   The notation of an out-cue of image change or audio cue for the end of a shot or a change of lighting is recorded here.

- **Audio Plot Form**

Production process   Talk show/entertainment program preproduction

Responsibility   Audio director

Purpose   To facilitate and encourage the design of sound perspective and recording for program production.

Objective   The audio plot form is designed to prompt the audio director to weight the set environment and sound production values in the planning for audio equipment and quality microphone pickup and recording during videotaping. The audio plot form is intended to encourage preproduction by the audio director.

Glossary

Audio Director   The name of the audio director is placed here.

Producer Approval   The audio director is required to get the approval of the producer for the audio plot. The producer's approval authorizes the expenses to be incurred for audio coverage of the production.

Program Title   The title of the program is listed here.

Date   The date the plot was designed is entered here.

Set   The set for which the audio plot is designed is listed here.

Page of   This notation indicates the total number of pages of the audio plot and carries the individual page number.

Sound: Synchronous/Silent   These choices of sound recording needs indicate what would be required on the set by the audio director. Synchronous sound indicates that both audio and video will be recorded during a portion of videotaping; silent means that video only is required (e.g., during playback of prerecorded tracks).

Microphone: Directional/Wireless/Other   The audio director chooses the kinds of microphones to be used during videotaping.

Microphone Support: Fishpole/Giraffe/Handheld/Hanging/Other   The audio director indicates the proposed microphone supports for sound coverage during studio production.

Foldback/Other   Here the audio director indicates what effects (e.g., studio foldback) are required.

Bird's Eye Floor Plan   The best preproduction information for the audio director is the floor plan for the set with talent and guest(s) movement indicated. The floor plan should be sketched in this box from the camera blocking form. Where the cameras are placed is important to the audio director, sound design, and microphone and microphone boom/grip placement during production.

Sound Perspective: Close/Distant   A change in camera framing could trigger a change in sound perspective, so the change in framing should be calculated in the basic sound design. The new framing composition is indicated by checking the appropriate symbols for new framing. Quality sound perspective creates the auditory sense that when talent is framed closely, sound levels should be higher; when talent and guest(s) are framed at a distance, sound levels should be lower.

Description   Any director's notes on the elements of the studio production of the program that will affect sound design and recording should be noted here. For example, excessive movement of talent and guest(s) or properties and expressive gestures could affect sound recording and control on the studio set. The fact that some sound playback may be required during a take would be noted here.

In-cue   The in-cue, from either visual imaging or audio cues, can affect the sound design of a take. That in-cue should be noted here.

Out-cue   The out-cue or final words of audio or a visual image can affect sound design. Notation of that cue should be made here.

- **Sound Effects/Music Plot Form**

Production process   Talk show/entertainment program preproduction

Responsibility   Audio director

Purpose   To summarize an audio effects and music breakdown of the proposed program.

Objective   The sound effects/music plot form is designed to categorize and summarize three types of audio preparation elements considered necessary to rehearsal(s) and videotape production of the program: sound effects and music needs, rights and clearances required, and a list of prerecorded audio tracks to be created.

Glossary

Audio Director   The name of the audio director of the new program is entered here.

Producer   The name of the producer of the program is recorded here.

Approval   A major reason for preparing this audio plot is to gain approval from the producer for the required effects and music for the new program. The audio director submits this completed form to the producer for approval. The producer indicates approval of the plot and authorization to purchase any needed resources.

Program Title   The title of the new program is indicated here.

Program Length   The telecast length of the new program is recorded here.

Date   The date of the composition of this plot is entered here.

Summary of Program Effects/Music Needs   This area of the plot lists those special effects and music proposed for the new program.

Effect   An effect can be a particular sound effect in the traditional sense (e.g., a drum roll) or an electronic sound (e.g., a recorded note from an electronic keyboard).

Music This column should note if and what music may be needed and proposed as a part of the program format (e.g., opening theme or bumper to commercials).

Source The source of either an effect or music entry in this row should also indicate from what audio playback source it will be (e.g., cartridge or videotape).

Length The required length needed for the program, not necessarily the total length of the effect or music source, should be recorded here.

Program Format Cues The audio director indicates from the program format sheet what cues within the program signal in-cue and out-cue for the respective effect or music.

Rights/Clearances This area is important to the program and the producer. The audio director indicates here what rights and clearances will be required from the copyright owners for permission to use a copyrighted effect or music proposed for the program. It is the responsibility of the producer to secure the respective clearances needed for the program.

Copyrighted Material The audio director records the particular material, either effect or music, that is proposed, but is copyrighted.

Publisher The name and address of the publisher of the copyrighted material are listed here. Note that publishers of copyrighted material do not necessarily hold the copyright for the material.

Copyright Owner The name and address of the owner of the copyright for the desired materials should be recorded here.

Clearances Needed The audio director should know what kind of clearance is needed from a copyright owner in order to use the material. For example, a common clearance requirement in television (and film) is synchronization rights for music.

Prerecorded Audio Tracks This area of the form lists any audio tracks that will have to be recorded before rehearsal(s) and videotaping of the program begin (e.g., announcer voice-over of opening copy).

Content/Copy The particular content (e.g., opening music theme) or copy (e.g., announcer copy) is indicated here.

Writer/Composer The copy writer or music composer of the content is indicated here.

Narrator/Artist The person performing the content or copy is listed here. That person may be a narrator for announcer copy or a vocalist for music.

Recorded This column permits the audio director to indicate that a particular prerecorded track is already recorded or to keep a record of when a track was recorded.

● **Character Generator Copy Form**

Production process Talk show/entertainment program preproduction

Responsibility Producer

Purpose To collect in one form all of the character generator copy for the program.

Objective The character generator copy form is the master list of all character generator copy to be entered into the memory of the character generator by the production assistant before program production begins. This master list is exhaustive and contains all copy for academy leader, program opening, program content, and closing credits for the program.

Glossary

Producer The name of the producer of the program is entered here.

Program Title The title of the proposed television program is entered here.

Production Date The date of the individual program production is entered here.

Page of The total number of expected pages for the character generator copy form is indicated here as is each individual page number.

Date This is the date on which the character generator form was prepared.

Production Assistant The name of the production assistant whose responsibility it will be to enter the copy into the character generator's memory is listed here.

Slate For programs recorded on videotape, which most are, some academy leader copy will have to be recorded.

Storyboard Frames This form includes aspect ratio frames designed to be typed in by the producer for maximum clarity. The form has to be read by the production assistant. There are plenty of blank frames. Each storyboard frame has three lines in the upper right hand corner in which to label the contents of the storyboard frame.

Record No. This box should contain the character generator screen page number for screen recall during production.

Closing Credits The closing credits pages of this form follow in the style of general character generator copy pages. These frames prompt names and roles of producers and production crew personnel as well as general television program credits. They may be used as they are or altered for a unique program.

Record No. Record number boxes are attached to these frames also to record the character generator screen page number for recall during production.

● **Format/Rundown Sheet Form**

Production process Talk show/entertainment program production

Responsibility Producer

Purpose To create and define the elements of each program videotaping session and the order and description of the production of those elements during studio videotaping.

Objective The studio format/rundown sheet creates the design of each program unit. The form contains the segments of the program and the breaks that separate the segments. The format/rundown sheet also indicates the order of the segments and elements of the program.

Glossary

Segment   This defines the program segments separated by breaks that make up the individual program format.

Contents   This area defines those differing elements that will make up the program. The contents area lists the guest(s), character generator copy, and a brief description of each element.

Time   This area defines the time of individual elements within the program's segments. These entries will sum up the elements of each program unit and, added to the time of the breaks, will sum up to the length of the program.

Running Time   This is the continuous time of the program beginning with zero.

Back Time   This is the continuous time of the program beginning with the length of the program (e.g., 28:30) and subtracting elements of the program to zero, the end of the program.

Opening   This area defines the first segment of the program. The other sequential segments—one, two, three, and closing—make up the set of segments for the specific program.

Notes   This area of the form describes specific elements of the segment that make up the content of the segment.

Commercial Break   These breaks comprise the proposed opportunities within the program format for commercials or public service announcements and their specific times.

• **Director's Checklist Form**

Production process   Talk show/entertainment program production

Responsibility   Director

Purpose   To organize pretaping studio roles and processes for the director and indicate problems and difficulties to be corrected during program critique sessions or production meetings.

Objective   The director's checklist form records the time of readiness for each studio production crew member and any reasons for delay and where in the process it occurs. The units of the checklist are job specific. A record of problems and reasons for delay in getting ready for production can be addressed at a critique session or later production meeting.

Glossary

Director   The name of the director of the program is entered here.

Program Title   The title of the program being produced is entered here.

Taping Date   The date of the production videotaping session is recorded here.

Production Job Title/Role   Each unit of this form provides a different job title or role description for production crew members involved in studio production. Each records the respective production personnel member.

Ready/Time   This records for the director the time that the particular production crew member indicated readiness for production.

Problem(s)/Delay   The director can indicate in this area of the form the particular problem or delay in getting ready. This will assist in trouble-shooting at a later time.

Production Meeting Notes   This area of the form permits the director the opportunity to make notes about production preparation that can be addressed at a later production meeting in an attempt to improve production preparation.

Glossary

Above-the-line Above-the-line is a division of television production personnel, often used for budgeting purposes, that distinguishes those who are in producing and nontechnical roles from those in strictly technical roles (below-the-line).

Academy leader The academy leader is the first minute of video preceding the content video of a recorded videotape. It consists of 30 seconds of color bars and audio tone, followed by 20 seconds of the slate of the content of the program, then by 10 seconds of black screen, and, finally, by the opening of the videotaped program.

Action props Action properties are those moving objects used by talent in production. For example, an automobile or horse and buggy are considered action properties.

Ambience Ambience is any background sound(s) in a recording environment; e.g., city traffic or an airplane flyover.

A-roll An A-roll video is the primary videotape playback source. In a studio production videotape environment, the A-roll playback is an edited master videotape to be inserted into a program. B-roll is a secondary videotape source that is inserted into the program record videotape. In postproduction, the A-roll is one of two source videotapes required to perform any mix of video effects, such as a dissolve.

Aspect ratio frame An aspect ratio frame is the television screen proportional rectangle drawing, 3 units high by 4 units long. Aspect ratio frames are drawings used in the design of storyboards.

Audience demographics Audience demographics is the sum of the individual traits of an audience; e.g., age, sex, education, income, race, and religion.

Audio perspective Audio perspective is the perception that longer video shots should have a more distant sound and closer video shots should have a closer sound. Audio perspective attempts to recreate the sound distance perception of real life.

Audio plot An audio plot is a preproduction task requirement of an audio director, which includes the judgment of type of microphone to record required sound of a production, microphone holder for picking up required sound, and physical placement of a microphone for a videotape shoot. (See the audio plot form.)

Audition An audition is the forum in which prospective talent try out for a part in a television production. Auditions can be used for any on-camera talent role; e.g., anchor for a newscast or host for a talk show.

Prospective talent should attend an audition with a vita or résumé of experience and a black-and-white glossy picture of him- or herself. During auditions, prospective talent may be asked to read a portion of a script, to improvise, or to characterize a situation or character.

Below-the-line Below-the-line is a division of television production personnel that distinguishes those who are involved in the production on a technical level from those who are involved on a nontechnical level (above-the-line). This division is used primarily for budgeting purposes.

Bird's eye view A bird's eye view is the point of view of a set looking directly down on the set from above, noting the confines of the set and set properties. The view can also contain the cast and the camera(s).

Bite A bite is a portion of a video or audio recording actuality.

Blocking Blocking is that process by which a director physically moves participants (cast and camera(s)) to differing points within a location or studio set.

Blocking plot Preparing a blocking plot is the preproduction task of a director, which consists of making a bird's eye view drawing of a set or recording environment with major properties indicated. A director indicates with circles where talent will be placed. The circles are combined with arrows to indicate movement of talent. From a blocking plot, a lighting director can create a lighting plot, and a camera operator can decide camera set-up and placement. (See the camera blocking plot form.)

Boom microphone A boom microphone is a microphone, usually directional, designed to be mounted and held above the person(s) speaking. A boom microphone must be aimed at the mouth of the speaker and raised and lowered depending on the camera framing of each camera shot. (*See also* Audio perspective.)

Breakdown A breakdown is a preproduction analysis of either a script or a storyboard. It is intended to separate scene elements from the script or storyboard and arrange them in proposed videotaping order. A breakdown is a necessary component to the development of a production schedule.

Bridge A bridge is a video or audio segment that connects, often in summary form, one video or audio subject to another.

B-roll A B-roll is a secondary videotape source needed in videotape production to perform some video effects involving two video sources during videotaping or editing, such as a dissolve or a special wipe effect. The A-roll would be the primary videotape source into which a B-roll source is inserted.

Cast call   The cast call is the designated time at which the members of the cast—talent and guest(s)—in a television production assemble before beginning production tasks.

Character generator   A character generator is a video effects generator that electronically produces text on a video screen. The text that is recorded in the memory of the character generator is usually used for purposes of matting over a color background or other video image.

Clearance   Clearance is the process of securing the rights to use copyrighted material. Clearance is most often secured for the legal use of music.

Clipsheet   A clipsheet is a summary form of information about an edited master videotape. Clipsheets list such information as the title of an edited master video piece, the length of edited video, the character generator copy to be matted over the video during the telecast, and the in-cues and out-cues of the video.

Composition of a shot   The composition of a camera shot indicates the subject and arrangement of a shot as framed in the viewfinder of a camera. It would indicate the person or object to be framed and the degree of the framing; e.g., CU or XLS.

Contingency   Contingency is that percentage amount added to a subtotal of estimated costs in budget making. A common contingency amount is 15% (i.e., 15% of the subtotal of estimated budget costs is added to the subtotal itself as a hedge against actual costs).

Continuity   Continuity is the flow of edited images and the content details of edited images from shot to shot. Continuity observation entails the close scrutiny of talent, properties, and environment during video recording to ensure accurate flow of edited images in postproduction.

Contrast ratio   Contrast ratio is the proportion of light to dark areas in electronic video images or across lighted areas on a set.

Control track   The control track is a flow of electronic impulses recorded on the edge of videotape that serve as synchronization units for accurate videotape editing. They serve the same purpose as the sprocket holes do on film.

Copy   Copy refers to any scripted text to be recorded on the audio track of a videotape or text recorded in the memory of a character generator for matting on a video image or background.

Copyright   Copyright is the legal right of an artist or author to the exclusive control of the artist's or author's original work. Copyrighted material is protected by law, and the public use of such material must always be cleared by a producer from the owner of the copyright.

Cover shot or camera   A cover shot or camera is usually the middle camera in a three camera live television production and is usually framed on a long shot to cover the set and talent. It is a camera shot the director can cut to while the other two cameras are reframing.

A cover camera may even be locked down on a long shot without an operator.

Credits   Credits are those on-screen texts that list the names and roles played or performed by all members of the crew and cast of the videotape production.

Crew call   A crew call is the stated time for the rendezvous of the production team members and is usually at a videotaping site.

Cross-camera design   Cross-camera design refers to the technique of multiple camera coverage of a production set in which the extreme right and left cameras cover the opposite areas of the set. For example, camera 1, positioned on an audience left side of a studio, covers the audience right side of the set; camera 3, on an audience right side of a studio, covers the audience left side of the set.

Cut-away   A cut-away is a video of related but extraneous content inserted into the primary video. For example, video images of a hospital operating room (related but extraneous) would serve as a cut-away insert to a video of an interview (primary video material) with a doctor.

Cut-in   A cut-in is a video of necessary and motivated video images to be edited into an established or master scene. For example, close-up shots (necessary and motivated) of two people in conversation serve as cut-ins to a long shot (master scene) of the two people walking and talking.

Cyclorama   A cyclorama is the ceiling to floor material used as a simple backdrop for some television studio productions. Cycloramas may be made of a black velour to provide a solid black background or a scrim material that may be lighted with any colored light.

Decibel   A decibel is a unit of sound that measures the loudness or softness of the sound.

Edited master   An edited master is the final editing of a video piece from source tapes.

External video signal   The external video signal is the control room signal that carries the program or line of the video program. In some studio operations, that signal can be routed to the individual studio cameras and called up by camera operators on their respective cameras. Having access to the external video signal allows camera operators to match the camera framing over their monitors to the camera framing as seen on the monitor of a camera on line.

Final audio   Final audio is used to designate the last sound of copy material or music in a video piece. It is a designated end point to measure the length of time of an edited master video piece. (*See also* First audio.)

Final edit   The final edit is the completed master tape of a video project. It is usually referred to in contrast to the rough edit, which is a preliminary videotape editing.

First audio   First audio is used to designate the first sound of copy material or music in a video piece. It is a designated beginning point to measure the length of time of an edited video piece. (*See also* Final audio.)

Fishpole   A fishpole is an extendible holder for a directional microphone. A fishpole, usually handheld, is extended into a set during dialogue for videotaping.

Foldback   Foldback is the process of feeding the audio signal of a studio production back into the studio for the convenience of studio personnel and on-camera talent.

Format   A format in video production is the listed order or outline of the content of a video product or program. Format is also used to indicate the genre of a television program, e.g., talk show or newscast.

Framing   Framing is the composition and degree of image arrangement as seen through the viewfinder of a camera. The framing is usually described in terms of how close or far away the subject is perceived to be from the camera; e.g., a close-up or a long shot. Camera framing involves the process of visualization.

Freelancer   A freelancer is a person who works in the film or video field on a production basis as opposed to being a full time employee. Writers, producers, and directors are examples of freelancers.

Freeze   A freeze in video production is the appearance of holding the video image on the screen still. A freeze is also used for production cast members when they must remain without movement while continuity notes are being made.

Friction   Friction, usually pan and tilt friction, refers to the amount of drag that the pan or tilt mechanisms produce in performing their functions. Adequate friction gives a camera operator control of panning and tilting motions.

F-stop   The f-stop units, the calibrated units on the aperture of the lens of a camera, determine the amount of light entering the lens and falling on the pickup tubes.

Gels   Gels (gelatin) are filters used in the control of light for videotaping. Gels are used on lighting instruments to filter light or change lighting temperature and on windows to change the temperature of light entering a videotaping environment.

Guest policy   Guest policy refers to those standards and criteria for guest appearances on a television program. Guest policy includes a guest fact sheet, biography, and booking and appearance schedule.

Hand properties   Hand properties are those objects needed (handled) by talent in television production. An example of a hand property would be a telephone.

In-cue   An in-cue is the beginning point of copy, music note(s), or video screen at which timing or video or audio inserting is to occur. (*See also* Out-cue.)

Insurance coverage   Insurance coverage is required for the use of certain people (e.g., underage children or movie stars), facilities (e.g., television studio or remote locations), and properties (e.g., horses or automobiles).

Intercom network   An intercom (intercommunication) network is that system of two-way communication through which television production crew members can interface with each other during studio production sessions.

Interviewee   An interviewee is the person being interviewed.

Interviewer   The interviewer is the person who interviews.

Lead   A lead indicates the beginning video and/or audio of a videotape piece. Leads may be created as a voice-over, as a stand-up, or with music.

Leader   The leader is the beginning portion of audio or videotape that is used to record information about the subsequent video or audio. Most leaders (often called academy leaders) contain the record of the slate and an audio check (e.g., :30 of tone) with a portion of video black before the principal video content of the recording. Some leaders also contain a portion of the color bars.

Legal clearance   Legal clearance is the process by which recording and reproduction rights are obtained to use copyrighted materials. Legal clearance must be obtained for copyrighted materials (e.g., for music, photographs, or film) and for synchronization (putting pictures to copyrighted music).

Levels   Levels are those calibrated input units of light, sound, and video that have to be set to record at acceptable degrees of unity and definition for broadcast reproduction purposes.

Lighting design   The lighting design is the preproduction stage during which the mood, intensity, and degree of light for a videotape production is created. The lighting design is the responsibility of the lighting director of a production. The lighting design can be done after location scouting is complete. (See the set lighting plot form.)

Location   A location is that environment outside a recording studio in which some videotaping is to be done, often referred to as the remote location or, simply, the remote.

Location log   The location log is the record of all video-taping done on location. The log contains notations about each videotaped take during a remote shoot. The location log serves as the editing cue sheet before postproduction editing.

Logging   Logging is the term used to indicate the process of keeping the location log. Logging is also used to record continuity details during a videotaped shoot.

Lower third   A lower third is the designation for the placement of character generator text copy on the television screen. The lower third is the bottom third of the television screen space where identifying names and titles are usually placed.

Master script   A master script is the copy of the script for a production that contains the preproduction information for a videotape shoot. The master script is usually the director's copy and contains the final version of the copy, the storyboard, and the blocking of actors and action props.

Master tape   A master tape is the videotape containing an edited video project.

Mike grip   A mike (microphone) grip is the individual responsible for holding the microphone or a microphone holder during the recording of audio in a studio or on location.

Mixing Mixing is the process of combining two or more audio tracks into one. Mixing usually adds music or ambient sound to a track of voice recording. Mixing audio tracks in videotape editing means to combine two recorded audio tracks into one audio channel.

Out-cue An out-cue is the end point of copy, music note(s), or video screen at which timing or video or audio inserting is to end. (*See also* In-cue.)

Pacing Pacing in an audio or video production is the perception of timing of the piece. Pacing is not necessarily the actual speed of a production or production elements, but it is the coordinated flow and uniformity of sequencing of all production elements; e.g., music beat, copy rhythm, or video cutting.

Package A package is the term used for the production of short video pieces. It is often synonymous with soft news video production.

Pad Pad (padding) is a term applied in television production whenever some flexible video, audio, black signal, or time may be needed.

Pickup pattern Pickup pattern designates the sound sensitive area around the head of a microphone. It is the area within which sounds will be heard by the microphone.

Pickup shots Pickup shots refers to the practice of videotaping additional studio set footage beyond scripted units to be used during postproduction editing. Pickup shots often will be used as cut-aways to cover difficult edits or mismatched edits discovered during editing. Pickup shot subject matter could be anything from a close-up of hands to a set table, an unopened door, or an attentive actor.

Picturization Picturization refers to the sequence of video images created through a production switcher. It includes the sequence of images and the transition between them (e.g., a cut or dissolve).

Pilot A pilot is a videotaped sample of a proposed television program.

Platform boom A platform boom is a large device for holding a microphone and extending it into a set during videotaping. Most platform booms are on wheels, need to be steered when moved, and require at least two operators—one to handle the microphone and the boom on the platform and the other to move the platform.

Plot A plot is a creative and/or technical design usually used for blocking actors within sets, designing sound coverage in audio production, designing the lighting pattern on sets, and listing all properties for a teleplay.

Preproduction script A preproduction script is a copy of a script for a video project that is considered subject to change. A preproduction script should contain sufficient audio and video material on which to judge the substance of the final proposed project.

Primary motion Primary motion is the movement in front of a television camera. It refers mainly to the movement of the talent.

Production meeting A production meeting is a gathering of all production personnel to go over details of a production.

Production statement A production statement is a simple, one sentence expression of the goal or objective of a videotape production. The production statement is a constant reminder at all stages of production of exactly what is being accomplished and why.

Production value A production value is any element or effect of a medium that is used when motivated to create an overall impact. Some examples of production values are music, lighting, and special video effects.

Program format A program format refers to the content and the order of that content in a television program. Format can also refer to the genre of the program; e.g., talk show or musical.

Prompter A prompter refers to either the production crew member who is responsible for coaching talent during production or the hardware used to project the script copy of a production to the front of the television cameras to assist the talent in reading.

Property Property is the term used for any movable article on a set. Properties include furniture, lamps, telephone, food, or bicycle. Properties are also classified as set, hand, and action.

Proposal A proposal is the set of preproduction elements used to present the idea and request for a video production. Most proposals require at least a treatment and a budget. A proposal might also contain a preproduction script and a storyboard.

Rate card A rate card is the list of space, hardware, personnel, services, and the cost for media production facilities.

Record button The record button is a circular red insert plug found on the bottom of most videotape cassettes. Removing the record button serves as a safety check against recording over or erasing previously recorded video material. The absence of the record button will allow playback, but not recording functions.

Roll tape "Roll tape" is the expression used to signal operation of the videotape recorder at the beginning of a videotape take. A location director uses the expression as a sign of his intention to videotape a scene.

Royalty Royalty is the share of proceeds from the publication of some work of art, such as a book, a play, or music. The performance of such works requires financial payment to the owner of the work.

Safety shot or camera A safety (or cover) shot or camera is usually the middle camera in a three camera live television production. The camera is usually framed on a long shot of the set and talent as a camera shot to which a director might cut while the other cameras are reframing.

Script unit A script unit is that section of a production script that designates a videotaping portion and is similar to a scene in a larger act. It is any gratuitous unit that a director may define for production purposes. Many professional scripts number all script units consecutively in right and left margins.

Secondary motion   Secondary motion refers to those movements in television that occur with the movement of the camera in production. Secondary movements include pan, tilt, dolly, truck, arc, zoom, pedestal, and boom.

Serendipity syndrome   The serendipity syndrome refers to those good and pleasant effects in television production that were unplanned and unexpected.

Shading   Shading in video production is the control of the iris of the lens of a video camera. It is the process of setting and/or controlling the iris for permitting or excluding light from hitting the camera tubes.

Shoot   A shoot is a slang term used to describe a videotape production session either on location or in the studio.

Shooting order   The shooting order is the order in which a production schedule indicates the script units will be shot during production. Most often, the shooting order is determined by the availability of locations and actors.

Shooting units   Shooting units refer to those portions of a television script that are producible in one continuous videotape take. Shooting units in television are similar to short scenes in theater. In commercial production, shooting units are determined by lines of script. In drama production, a shooting unit is determined by pages of script or portions of a page.

Shot list   The shot list is a form created during preproduction in which a director indicates types and order of shots to be videotaped during location production. A shot list differentiates between master or establishing shots and cut-ins, provides framing instructions, and indicates the duration of each shot by out-cue. Shot lists are location specific with the shot list for every location beginning with the count of one.

Slate   The slate is an audio and video recording device that allows the labeling of the leader of each videotape take. A slate usually records the title of the production, producer and/or director, date, take number, and videotape code. The character generator can serve as a slate as can a blackboard or white showcard. Slate also indicates the action of recording the slate on the videotape leader.

SMPTE time code   SMPTE (Society of Motion Picture and Television Engineers) time code is an electronic signal recorded on a secondary audio track of videotape stock to assist an editor in accurately creating a videotape edit. SMPTE time code records the hours, minutes, seconds, and frame numbers of elapsed time for each video frame.

Soft news   Soft news is that news event that is not necessarily recent or time sensitive. It is referred to as evergreen or timeless.

Sound coverage   Sound coverage is the process of determining how television production environments can be covered by microphones for sound recording.

Sound effects   Sound effects are those prerecorded sounds that simulate sounds in the real environment. They are used to create a lifelike environment in the television studio and for background to a dialogue track in drama production.

Source tape   The source tape is any videotape stock used to record video that will later be edited into a larger videotape project. Source tapes are edited onto a master tape.

Spike marks   Spike marks are the result of spiking cast or properties during television production. A common form of spike marks are colored adhesive dots placed at the blocked positions of talent and guest(s). A different colored dot is assigned to each cast member.

Spiking   Spiking in television production is the process of recording with some form of marking the blocked position of a cast member, set property, or studio camera.

Stand-by   Stand-by is a verbal command that indicates the director is ready to begin videotaping a location unit. Production and crew respond to a stand-by command with silence and readiness to begin.

Storyboard   A storyboard is a series of aspect ratio frame forms used to sketch the proposed composition and framing of each shot to be videotaped for a production. Storyboard frames are numbered consecutively, and the audio copy associated with each proposed shot is recorded under the frame. Storyboards are considered essential to some video genres (e.g., commercials) and are encouraged as a quality preproduction stage for all genres.

Strike   A strike is the final stage of a location shoot when all videotape production equipment is disassembled and packed for removal and the shooting environment is restored to the arrangement and condition found at the arrival of the production crew.

Synchronization rights   Synchronization rights are those legal clearances in which a producer receives the right to use copyrighted music in a videotape production.

Take   A take is a single videotape unit from the beginning to the end of recording. A take usually begins with a recording of the slate and ends with a director's call to cut. It is not uncommon to record many takes of an individual unit. Many takes may be required for one shot.

Talent   Talent is the term used to designate any person who appears in front of a camera, both actors and extras. Even animals are referred to as talent.

Talent release   Talent release is a signed legal document by which a producer obtains the rights to use the image, voice, and talent of a person for publication.

Target audience   Target audience is the designation of that subset of the public for whom a particular video piece is designed. Knowing a target audience permits a producer and director to make calculated choices of production values to attract and hold the interest of the targeted group.

Tertiary motion   Tertiary motion in television production refers to the appearance of movement effected by the production switcher; e.g., a cut between video images or a dissolve across images.

Timing   Timing is the process of recording the length of a video piece from first to final audio. First audio and final audio might be music and not a vocal cue. Some video pieces may have a visual cue at the beginning or end of the piece.

Titling Titling is the design and production of all those on-screen visual elements that create the title of a video production.

Treatment A treatment is a preproduction stage in which a producer describes a proposed video production for the purpose of soliciting approval to go into production with the project. The treatment may include a synopsis of a story, the goal and objective of a video piece, and the audience's need for the production. (See the program treatment form.)

Vectorscope A vectorscope is an oscilloscope used to set and align the color of images as they are recorded by the videotape recorder.

Videographer A videographer is a photographer working in video.

Visualization Visualization is the process of creating video images of an environment—people, objects, and events. Visualization is translated into camera and lens framing techniques.

Voice-over A voice-over is a production technique in which an announcer's voice is heard without the announcer being seen in the video portion. A voice-over is a common technique in news reporting. Leads, bridges, and tags may all be produced as voice-overs.

Wrap A wrap is the stage of a studio videotape production when the director indicates that a good take has been videotaped and signals a move to another shot from the shot list. A wrap is distinguished from a strike.

Selected Bibliography

Armer, A. *Directing Television and Film, Second Edition.* Belmont, CA: Wadsworth Publishing Co., 1990.

Blum, R. A. *Television Writing from Concept to Contract, Revised Edition.* New York: Hastings House, 1984.

Blumenthal, H. J. *Television Producing & Directing.* New York: Harper & Row, 1988.

Carlson, V., and Carlson, S. *Professional Lighting Handbook.* Stoneham, MA: Focal Press, 1985.

Fielding, K. *Introduction to Television Production.* New York: Longman, 1990.

Fuller, B., Kanaba, S., and Kanaba, J. *Single Camera Video Production: Techniques, Equipment, and Resources for Producing Quality Video Programs.* Englewood Cliffs, NJ: Prentice Hall, 1982.

Garvey, D., and Rivers, W. *Broadcast Writing.* New York: Longman, 1982.

Huber, D. M. *Audio Production Techniques for Video.* Indianapolis, IN: Howard Sams & Co., 1987.

Hubatka, M. C., Hull, F., and Sanders, R. W. *Sweetening for Film and TV.* Blue Ridge Summit, PA: TAB Books, 1985.

Kehoe, V. *Technique of the Professional Make-up Artist.* Stoneham, MA: Focal Press, 1985.

Kennedy, T. *Directing the Video Production.* White Plains, NY: Knowledge Industry Publications, Inc., 1988.

Mathias, H., and Patterson, R. *Achieving Photographic Control over the Video Image.* Belmont, CA: Wadsworth Publishing, Co., 1985.

McQuillin, L. *The Video Production Guide.* Sante Fe, NM: Video Info, 1983.

Miller, P. *Script Supervising and Film Continuity.* Stoneham, MA: Focal Press, 1986.

Millerson, G. *Video Production Handbook.* Stoneham, MA: Focal Press, 1987.

Nisbett, A. *The Use of Microphones, Second Edition.* Stoneham, MA: Focal Press, 1983.

Schihl, R. J. *Single Camera Video: From Concept to Edited Master.* Stoneham, MA: Focal Press, 1989.

Souter, G. A. *Lighting Techniques for Video Production: The Art of Casting Shadows.* White Plains, NY: Knowledge Industry Publications, Inc., 1987.

Weise, M. *Film and Video Budgets.* Stoneham, MA: Focal Press, 1980.

Wiegand, I. *Professional Video Production.* White Plains, NY: Knowledge Industry Publications, Inc., 1985.

Utz, P. *Today's Video: Equipment, Set Up and Production.* Englewood Cliffs, NJ: Prentice Hall, 1987.

Verna, T., and Bode, W. *Live TV: An Inside Look at Directing and Producing.* Stoneham, MA: Focal Press, 1987.

Zettl, H. *Television Production Handbook, Fourth Edition.* Belmont, CA: Wadsworth Publishing Co., 1984.

Zettl, H. *Sight, Sound, Motion: Applied Media Aesthetics, Second Edition.* Belmont, CA: Wadsworth Publishing Co., 1990.

Index